The Bible
Answers Us with Pictures

The Bible Answers Us with Pictures

Christa Meves

Translated by Hal Taussig

Photographs by
Hal and Verena Taussig

The Westminster Press
Philadelphia

Translated from the German
Die Bibel antwortet uns in Bildern.
Tiefenpsychologische Textdeutungen im
Hinblick auf Lebensfragen heute

© Verlag Herder KG Freiburg im Breisgau 1973
Fifth edition, 1974

PUBLISHED BY THE WESTMINSTER PRESS®
PHILADELPHIA, PENNSYLVANIA

PRINTED IN THE UNITED STATES OF AMERICA

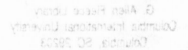

Library of Congress Cataloging in Publication Data

Meves, Christa.
  The Bible answers us with pictures.

  Translation of the 5th ed. of Die Bibel antwortet uns
in Bildern.
  1. Bible—Psychology. I. Title.
BS645.M4813   220.6   76–49909
ISBN 0–664–24130–1

Contents

Preface

What an exciting and promising achievement this book is! Christa Meves, trained in psychology and a practicing psychotherapist, has contributed to one of the most important tasks of the twentieth-century church—the rediscovery of the Scriptures. By applying depth psychological understanding to Biblical images, she simultaneously illuminates the meaning of the text in its original historical context and for today's readers.

These accomplishments have provoked excited response in Germany, where demand for the book required five printings in its first eighteen months.

Frau Meves is well known in German-speaking Europe for her numerous books in psychology and education, but in this volume she has gathered many experiences from her counseling practice and related them to the interpretation of the Bible. Her contribution extends beyond a compatibility with the general theological drift of our time and speaks directly to several contemporary issues in Biblical studies. By showing the essentially irreducible character of a series of Biblical symbols and by comparing them to the dreams of modern Western persons, she demonstrates how the mythical images of the Bible can and do function in the contemporary psyche, and so opens the way for further reappropriation of the mythical language of the Bible.

The author's mode of interpretation, moreover, can go even beyond the limits she has set for herself. For instance, her interpretation of the parables is really much more promising than she gives herself credit for. She limits herself to those parables which are not "interpreted" by Jesus. Current scholarship, however, encourages a separation of the parable from the allegorical "interpretation" that most probably was given to it later. Thus, one could apply her mode of interpretation to many more parables, while still respecting the original intent of Jesus.

Similarly, this kind of interpretation has promise for a much wider range of Biblical materials. As Frau Meves notes in her introduction, she has gravitated toward the texts that seemed easiest or most obvious to her. Consequently, she seems to have chosen particularly those parts of the Biblical witness which accent order. The Biblical themes of freedom and release, however, also could have been developed and her mode of interpretation applied to the exodus, the psalms of praise, the Song of Songs, the Messianic titles, and the Pauline polemic against the law.

With the gracious permission of the author, I have translated quite freely. In addition to attempting to rework much of the Germanic style, I have occasionally omitted something. For instance, Frau Meves at one point maintained that protest against the Vietnam war was much more abstract than being humane to one's own family. This was undoubtedly much truer for the German protesters than for the Americans, who faced conscription and indeed family conflict because of the Vietnam war. So in my translation I have simply said that protest against a distant war is less immediate than the familial conflict.

In Scriptural quotations I have generally followed Frau Meves' preference in the German edition for the Jerusalem Bible. At many points, however, she does not use the Jerusalem Bible and the English Jerusalem Bible does not always relate adequately to her emphasis. I have therefore consulted the Greek or Hebrew text myself and in many instances provided my own translation.

Since the author's work is a call for us to take the significance of images more seriously, I have viewed the accompanying photography in this book as part of that greater task. The photographs, which my wife, Vreni, and I have done, are meant to encourage the superimposition of the imaged Biblical truths onto the contemporary human spirit. They are presented

8

as a part of the effort to revitalize the function of Biblical imagery.

The photographs are meant to function in two fairly distinct ways. Some of the pictures are meant simply to illustrate the assertion of the author or the Biblical text. These photographs picture in an obvious and straightforward manner the way the symbols discussed in the book function in our time. Other photographs are meant to create a metaphoric tension in support of Frau Meves' and the Bible's contention that some images are not entirely reducible. They invite the reader to dwell with the images themselves and to feel and contemplate their metaphoric power.

I am grateful to my wife, Vreni, for her consultations concerning my translation, and to Stephen Gibson for his work with the manuscript.

HAL TAUSSIG

Calvary United Methodist Church
Philadelphia, Pennsylvania

Introduction

"How can I make sense of it all?"

In a variety of forms this question has come over the past years with an unexpected intensity in my counseling practice and lectures. Repeatedly, questions have arisen about the meaning of one's own life, about the goal of development in human beings, about the origin and aim of existence. The amazing part of it is that I have not been directing myself to such personal or philosophical questions. But they have kept coming at me, who had been trained to deal with psychological and pedagogical issues.

Often I found myself answering these questions about the meaning of life with a word or a picture from the Bible. I tried to translate some Biblical passages into our logical and abstract modes of thinking. Most of the time that opened up a basic thirst for more. I began to sense an extraordinarily strong need for a better understanding of the ancient wisdom.

In the following pages I have addressed this need of my audience and readers, who seemed at points almost desperate. This book intends to help people grasp more clearly the language of pictures and the timeless truth shining through them in the Biblical stories. That means nothing other than banging loose a layer of cement which we have used to wall off the ancient springs of wisdom. We have indeed walled them off with the help of the rational-logical mode of thought, because we fancied that we no longer needed the ancient sources. But —to stay with picture language—the tree of our soul does not allow itself to be nourished with hard, calcium-laden tap water. It dies if we use such nourishment over a long period of time.

That basic thirst, which is our religious need, is satisfied only from the eternal streams of the depths. These streams also exist in each of us—as my image of the walled-off spring implies. We need only make the effort to free them. We each have—the world of images in our dreams proves it—a basic and immediate relationship to that world which lies beyond the conceptual and perceivable. In this picture world alone are also the answers to questions of meaning. For each person the meaning is there, relevant to each individual and therefore part of a larger, shared accord. Without this personal search for the answer to the question, What does this life of mine mean? we remain both poor and unequipped for the unavoidable crises and catastrophes of our life. The Bible can still negotiate an answer for us in the language of pictures. We need only learn to understand these images. A short time ago in my practice a young woman, after a number of suicide attempts and some time together with me, told me: "When things at home became so hard again, I might certainly have tried again to kill myself. But since you told me the story of Job, since I know that my endurance already has a meaning, suicide attempts don't get off the ground."

The following interpretations of Biblical texts have been written in the hope that they might be able to negotiate more help of this kind. For in my years of work with children and youth, in observing their dreams, their fantasies, and the unconscious content of their play, I have become aware of a creative productivity. This productivity unconsciously governs their minds and expresses itself in similar images and symbols. These same images are found in large number in the Bible also. I could understand what I experienced in astounding abundance with these Biblical images only as a view on the other side of reality, as an experience of God's doing. It was in this way that through my work came an understanding of symbols, an entry into Christianity, which also in my case had been blocked through faulty information. In my practice I learned how fundamentally valid the wisdom of the Bible is for us today. And through my work I also witnessed how an understanding of Biblical perception can be a decisive, available help in one's life. For humankind in earlier times such an experience was certainly possible without mediation. But we contemporary persons with our enlightened ego consciousness need the rugged detour through our intellect. That does not necessarily mean remaining stuck in some "demythologization" enterprise. Experience teaches that when ears are once again opened, a new dimension of understanding can begin. Once this happens, reflection is not necessary, because a new ability to recognize, an intuition of deep visionary dimensions, a new possibility of "seeing through," is in operation. In the healing process within psychotherapy too such things can happen through the enlivening of that dimension of depth in which the picture world of the soul finds its roots. In order to make this healing process clearer I have used a case of this kind in a special chapter (Chapter 8, "Psychic Healing and Religious Renewal").

The book contains only a small, even just a tiny, selection of Biblical texts. The selection was made in view of the possibilities of such an exemplary study. The stories that were picked are especially applicable to the methodology of depth psychology. They are to a certain extent selected to make visible certain aspects of image perception that have not been emphasized by theological exegetes. In no way does this study claim to have discovered the only valid interpretation.

The same applies to my interpretations of the archetypal images themselves. Jung has said: "One cannot for one second promote the illusion that an archetype could be finally explained and therefore done away with. Even the best attempts at clarification are nothing other than a more or less fortunate translation into another language of images." (Carl Gustav Jung and Karl Kerényi, *Einführung in das Wesen der Mythologie;* Amsterdam and Leipzig, 1941.)

A factor that influenced my choice of texts was my attempt to find passages that would bring understanding to certain problems of our age or that would encourage reflection on these contemporary problems. In this respect my practice directed me to the importance of the individual question about finding one's self and the social question concerning what kind of help is most effective. Here the parables of Jesus should be a starting place for reflection and problem-solving. Indispensable to this objective of mine became the undertaking of a detailed interpretative work on the last book of the Bible, the apocalyptic visions of John. In our age of compromise and veilings one is only too easily convinced to hush up the powerful admonition, the clear orientation, of this book. Whoever pushes aside the existence of these powers or endeavors to relegate them with a scornful arrogance to "one of the smallest" does not succeed in eliminating them from the world. Instead of minimizing or belittling these powers, ignoring them causes the particular person to be unprepared to deal with the assault of these powers. The revelations of John teach us of a great cosmic educational principle concerning constructive and fruitful learning through shock and horror. It teaches us that it would be arrogant to think that we can eliminate the positive function of fear. It is dangerous frivolity not to take seriously Christ's reference to the "wailing and gnashing of teeth" at the Last Judgment. That would be to think ourselves more papal than the pope and more able to behave humanely than Jesus. Fear and guilt are existential and fundamental phenomena. They do not let themselves be pushed aside any more than our vital drives, such as sexuality, allow themselves to go unrecognized. A humane counseling can free one from a sick guilt feeling rooted in a dictatorship of a scrupulous conscience. However, there is also justified fear, which has a life-preserving significance. There is a justified fear which warns us about skipping blindly into ruin.

In addition I have tried to choose Bible passages that bring into the foreground the basic and substantial motifs of the Biblical heritage. In the many hours of reading the Holy Scriptures which preceded this work, the Bible appeared to me like a great wonderful symphony, in which single themes repeated themselves again and again, either uncovered in powerful clarity or changed, modulated with undercurrents, like preludes drawn out through intervals, nevertheless in an artful, constructive order, as in the great Bach concertos. To direct attention to these themes in the Biblical symphony, to raise them up in a certain didactic manner, this has been my intent.

With reference to the use of this little book, I would like to recommend that the reader follow the text in its given order as much as possible. It seemed to me senseless to repeat in each chapter the depth psychological explanations or symbolic interpretations that had just been treated in the preceding pages.

I have cited the particular Biblical texts in full, with several minor exceptions where the train of thought would have been destroyed by full citation. My citations have been mostly from the Jerusalem Bible, and in several cases from the Luther Bible. In comparing certain points in each of the above translations, I observed glaring differences from time to time. In the face of these almost contradictory translations I felt lost. For example, the depth psychological symbolism of a calf (Luther) is completely different from that of a bull (Jerusalem Bible). In such cases I returned to the original language with the worthy help of my husband, who knows Greek, and the theologically aware biologist, Professor J. Illies. In the particular case of the calf vs. the bull, the Greek *moschos* means literally sprout—therefore, a young animal. Since the Greek usage indicated a younger animal, I decided that "calf" was the more justified translation.

In addition I want to thank Pastor Manfred Kiessig of Munich for looking through the manuscript with theologically critical eyes. My deep gratitude must also be expressed to my friend Charlotte Rosteck for her tireless attention to my typographical and stylistic errors.

This little book wants to stimulate in a decisive manner. It wants to work with the reader in pushing aside the patches of fog in the contemporary absence of orientation, in order that the grand and holy towers of light may again become visible.

CHRISTA MEVES

Uelzen, January 1973

1.

Expulsion as Motivation for Maturation:
A Depth Psychological Interpretation of the Fall
(Gen. 3:1-24)

Through their work with dreams, depth psychologists have come to a central recognition: there is a language of the soul, the basic unit of which is images. Our own fantasies and the unusual and puzzling dreams we have at night have taught us that our soul tells its own story in parables.

Yes, the human soul makes its sensitive areas known and unburdens itself in the process of awesome pressures. It announces a person's inner needs through dramatic premonitions. The soul stands ready with an array of counsel and strength to sound the alarm and to warn a person of impending conflict or difficulty.

Dreams are like a secret hot line which sends its messages in a certain code. Discovering the keys to this secret code has been one of the major tasks of doctors and psychologists since Freud rediscovered the code's existence and pointed out its importance in treating mental illness.

But then there was a great surprise. The dream researchers discovered that the ancient stories of humankind, the myths and the fairy tales, used the same kind of parabolic language. Upon closer examination one began to see that these ancient legends were also talking about the same events of the soul that contemporary dreams referred to. It was discovered that the ancient stories had reference not so much to certain historical events as to the timeless messages of the soul concerning its condition and development. Indeed, it seemed that often the myths contained *messages concerning the soul of a whole people,* not simply of an individual. Work with these symbolic pictures, this mythic mode, provides possibilities of seeing through the superficial appearances of life to a level of human life which "is deeper than the day." This world of dreams and myths with its profound promise is not graspable with our ordinary tools of reason. But with some "translation" their meaning becomes clearer.

The Genesis story in the Bible is a good example. Clearly it has little to do with a scientific or historical account of nature's beginnings. But its content becomes powerfully enlightening when one applies the principles of dream interpretation to it. Especially the work of C. G. Jung and its amplification and clarification in ethnological studies is of help here. Let us with the above help take one of the most impressive stories of Genesis, the story of the Fall, as the subject of such a "translation."

Before I begin, one further prefatory remark is needed. C. G. Jung taught that in the symbolic happenings of the soul's process so-called levels of subjectivity occur. That means that the various figures are not to be understood as individuals. Rather, these figures are personified functions of a larger psychic totality. They are aspects of the variety within the human soul itself. Seen in this way, the various figures symbolize certain parts of the soul. Several of the great romantic poets sensed this same quality of the human situation. Novalis, for instance, writes: "The person may be divided into a number of persons, while still maintaining a unified existence. The true analysis of the individual reveals a variety of persons. Individual personhood is simply the isolation, division, and disintegration of the multiplicity of persons."

When we take this approach to the story of the Fall, the text can be understood to describe a process of inner human development. Obviously the figure of the snake is not a cobra or a

18

viper or any actual member of that species, since the snake engages Eve in conversation. No scientist of any school would even want to try to prove that snakes once spoke human language. We can, rather, assume that this tempting voice of the snake is an "inner voice" in humans.

But what could it mean to present a part of the human psyche as a snake? In our work with dreams we have noted that this picture embodies certain qualities which accurately characterize a portion of the human soul. What kind of human qualities does the snake embody in this inner language?

We can assume that at the time of the composition of Genesis the snake had been observed quite carefully by men and women. The snake is an uncanny being. It lives in hidden places, and is quick and crafty when pursued. Its skin can transform and develop the snake's appearance through the removal of the old, dead, stiff and unusable skin. The phallus-like figure of the body and the head which brings death through injection of poison can become a symbol for a negative aspect of generative power. This symbol is confirmed both by contemporary dreams and ancient myths of various cultures.

From these givens we can conclude that the snake embodies a portion of human personhood that presses for change. This would be the part of us that stands against the given order of things, the desire in us to overcome our dependencies through craft or assertiveness. The snake represents the spirit of the revolution, the renegade in each of us. It is the human urge to realize a change in the fundamental ordering of life. Yes, the story is about this inner drive for grasping power for oneself. The text notes the words of the snake to Eve: "and you will become like gods, knowing good and evil."

This picture of the temptation to seize power and to be the renegade belongs to the very being of humankind. It has been demonstrated so many times in the lives of individuals and peoples that we can rightly see in this image an archetypal principle of human behavior. Not only in the revolutions of history, not only in the current liberation movements does the snake and its voice live. Such drives bear directly also on the developmental process of every child.

In every three-to-four-year-old boy, who with foot-stamping resists his parents' commands or in secret attempts to do something that has been forbidden, lies the spirit of the snake. Here too is the push for change, for loosing the fetters, for independence.

But before we deal with the results of this violation of commands, we need to treat the two human figures in the story—the man and the woman, Adam and Eve. In doing so, let us remain in the inner realm, understanding each figure to represent part of the human psyche. In each of us there lives the masculine and the feminine, no matter to which sex we belong by birth. That is, there are qualities in each of us which one has experienced since ancient times as specifically male or female. The dominance of knowledge, thinking, and logic count as masculine; the dominance of feeling, naturalness, beauty, approachability, and spontaneity count as feminine. The feminine in us, according to this Biblical story, stands in close relationship to natural powers, to instinct, impulse, and drives. For it is Eve whom the snake interrogates. Feeling (the Eve in us), the text seems to tell us, is desirous, instinctive, egotistic, and impulsive. It not only likes to look, it also likes to have and to possess. For that reason one reads in Genesis: "The woman saw that the tree was good to eat and to look at, and desirable in order to have knowledge."

There is still more wisdom about the feeling side of people in this passage. This side of the human psyche is a bit dull and can be led astray. As such, it desires perception and knowledge. Our feeling side is instinctively inquisitive and can easily thereby slip into dangerous borderline situations. This side of our being recalls the enthusiasm of small children who overlook danger in spite of warning—like small boys playing catch with a grenade they have unearthed. It also recalls the headlong curiosity of the research scientists who, without thought for consequences or humanitarian limits, throw themselves into the intellectual quest.

Is the masculine sleeping within us during such attacks? At least—the text seems to say—it is quite inactive. It receives the knowledge and is enlightened by it. But logic, one could say,

In every three- to four-year-old lies the spirit of the snake. Here too is the push for change, for loosing the fetters, for independence

neither stimulates nor enacts changed behavior. It remains inactive, in sleepy tolerance, yet positioned against the pressing and active part of the soul. That is, although thought represents the most highly developed aspect of creation, it alone can effect no change. Change—as the intrigue between the snake and Eve shows—is a matter of the bestial, the instinctive in combination with spontaneous readiness to act and a greedy drive to possess.

Change does not consist of reflection—that is a psychological given of indisputable truth. One can arrive at an additional insight with the help of experiences with the mentally ill. That insight is that people whose intellect dominates have a great need to reach some kind of spontaneous deal or decision. On the other hand, people in whom the spirit of Eve reigns unswervingly fall from one thoughtless adventure into another. However, people in whom only the spirit of the snake reigns are in danger of, through the poison of self-assertion, destroying themselves and their surroundings.

Now, Genesis reveals such a situation in which the power drive and spontaneity dominate. And Genesis also shows us the consequences. In the picture of the taking and eating from the tree of knowledge we see the representation of human behavior breaking out of the established boundaries. The "taking" of the fruit symbolizes the "understanding" formerly unavailable to humankind. Eating is an ancient mythical symbol for the incorporation and integration of new insight. Countless scientific discoveries, from the discovery of dynamite to the construction of the atom bomb to the insights into human physiology won through vivisection, are examples of this breaking out of the established boundaries.

But there are examples in our individual lives too. In every child the temptation of the snake is dramatized anew. The desire to discover is already there in four- and five-year-olds. They are driven to discover the secrets behind Santa Claus or the Easter bunny or their parents' moments of intimacy or the contents of a stuffed doll's stomach. Always the consequences of this surpassing of boundaries are the same, just as Genesis shows us.

The step beyond the established order produces a revelation. Disappointingly the discovery, however, is not that one is finally and fully in command. Rather, a guilt-ridden imperfection is revealed. Knowledge makes nakedness visible. In this nakedness one recognizes clearly one's own bestial drivenness. The snake in humankind shows itself as a part of Adam's body. This insight into the animal quality of our lives belongs to our recognition of God's creation. It becomes a sign of our imperfection, a blemish which we are ashamed of and try to cover up.

To see here only a statement about sexual drives would be reductionist. Adam and Eve's shame of their nakedness and their exposed genitals image the insight that humankind relates imperfectly to the drives in each person. Desires for food, possessions, power, and sex belong to these drives. Together they represent the dependent nature of human beings.

The snake in the human being, his drivenness, can lead him astray toward isolation and hiddenness from creation. Therefore the Genesis text rightly presents Eve's words: "The snake tempted me and I ate."

Processes of this sort occur anew in every epoch where a nature people reach the level of consciousness and see themselves over against nature. At the point where a people begin to explore nature and attempt to change it, there that people take the first step toward their own culture and into the process that Genesis symbolically describes.

But this is not just a social phenomenon. The same process happens to individuals. Five-to-six-year-olds are out of the stage of fascination with secrets. For them, the increasing distinction between self and world is accompanied by a new need —the need to cover oneself up, to avoid being seen naked. The child begins to be ashamed in front of others. The appearance of such tendencies in the child's development focuses us more clearly on what the story of the Fall is saying about the human situation. The raising of consciousness, the first step toward individuation, also initiates an isolation of the self and the dawning of a feeling of shame over the needful and drive-dominated imperfection within.

Reaching a new level of consciousness, which the eating of the forbidden fruit so aptly portrays, now effects a powerful change within the person. This change is pictured in Genesis in the punishment which God unlooses on the snake, Adam, and Eve. The snake is cursed beyond all animals of the field. Now it must crawl on its stomach and eat dirt. If we continue to interpret the snake as a part of the human soul, specifically as the spirit of instinctive grasping for power, then these words of God characterize the drive for power in humans as the most dangerous opponent of creation. Here the grasping for power is seen as more evil than all other drives in nature and in persons. The picture of crawling on one's stomach and eating dirt expresses wonderfully the insight that such self-assertion is connected to the realm of the material. Yes, this close connection to the matter of the drive can eventually be the means of evolving a tangible understanding of our drivenness.

Is this not a brilliant characterization of the countless over-steppings of boundaries by our modern natural sciences? Do we not know today that we need to be on our guard against the snake's arrogant claim to the powers of creation? Yes, we already know about eating dirt. Our culture has been arrested at the snake's level, where only the superficial, the shallow, and the material are perceivable.

How profound the curse of enmity between the snake and the woman becomes in this perspective. The offspring of the woman will crush the head of the snake, and the offspring of the snake will sting the heel of the woman. Does this mean that the spontaneity and instinct for perception of humankind will be able to undo the materialist domination, but that this victory will be illusory because material will cunningly revenge itself? In any case the dangers of unbounded research and the often belatedly visible revenge which nature takes as a result are obvious.

I believe that our subjective interpretation of the meaning of the curse on the woman can be especially enlightening. If we do not take the difficulty of pregnancy and the pains at birth literally, we move toward an understanding of that great step over the boundary into consciousness. If we see the image of the woman's punishment as a symbolic portrayal of the development of human feeling and consciousness, then we see clearly the meaning of the break from nature. This is the impulse in the human being which initiates constant transformation and painful processes of inner becoming. The image of pregnancy and birth shows that the overstepping of established boundaries leaves him between hoping and flinching, blood and tears, pains and pushings toward an unending process of change. The drive for self-empowerment results in the impulse to take on new skin, to movements of becoming, wasting away, and becoming again.

And seen in this subjective manner the words of God to Eve are not a proclamation of the value of the patriarchy. The words, "Your yearning will be for your husband, but he will rule over you," become fulfillment of the instinctive desire of feeling for completion through understanding. That is, the submission of feeling to the governing principle of understanding allows for a development which cannot happen with drives and impulsiveness alone. This lack of discipline of our feeling side, the text says, brings on its entanglement under the power of the intellect. And has not this prognosis of the overintellectualization of moderns with all its dangers been fulfilled in an all too demonic fashion?

The fate of Adam after God's punishment—for us, the fate of understanding—appears in his continual susceptibility to temptation by feeling. For God speaks to Adam:

Because you listened to the voice of your wife and ate from the tree of which I had forbidden you to eat, accursed be the soil because of you.

As for human understanding, the whisperings of the spirit of self-assertion and the drive for knowledge chain it to matter; they make the earth a cursed object in its hand. That is, the level of consciousness which human beings attain through self-assertion, a drive for knowledge, and reflection brings about their attachment to matter. This dependence on matter bestows a sad fate on human understanding. Its doings are full of hardship. The fruits of its knowledge are meager and untasteful, like the grass of the field. Its work is among thorns and thistles. The separation of the human being from his origin makes him a prisoner of matter, of the earth. This means that this part of the human being is left to die in matter. For that reason the text says: "For earth you are, and to earth you must return." But since self-assertion is a drive, and since drives are tied to matter, and since matter encompasses death, humankind cannot come to eternal life through self-assertion.

Disobedience makes expulsion from the spiritual and eternal natural unity with God unavoidable. For that reason Genesis reads:

> And the Lord God said, See, the man has become like one of us, with his knowledge of good and evil. He must not be allowed to stretch his hand out next and pick from the tree of life also, and eat some and live forever.
> So the Lord God expelled him from the garden of Eden, to till the soil from which he had been taken. He drove Adam out, and in front of the garden of Eden he posted the cherubs, and the flame of a flashing sword, to guard the way to the tree of life.

Every person experiences this garden of Eden, this oneness with God, in his prenatal and early postnatal life. Out of those early experiences everyone brings the more or less conscious desire for that security. The desire remains even after the person has achieved self-consciousness by means of understanding and the spirit of resistance. And every person also knows about the encounter with the cherub, the angel with the flaming sword, when he attempts to flee back into that sacred and deathless condition of unconsciousness.

When a human being tries to reject selfhood because life becomes too hard, he slips into the danger of being singed and wounded by the flaming sword of the angel. That is, whoever mutinies against going on with life becomes mentally ill, often even physically sick. That person sulks at the gates of paradise. At that point he slips into a stagnation of his own development. That is, he becomes wounded. There is no way back. This is

26

the message of the picture of the angel with the flaming sword. After the fall, after the separation from God, the only alternative is to accept the constant need for change.

Such is the story of the expulsion from paradise as seen through an understanding of depth psychology. The psychology of development confirms the truth of this ancient Biblical story. And perhaps this psychological perspective can make a few comforting observations about the meaning of this our human fate.

In working with mentally ill children and adolescents one gains the insight that the loss of the paradise of childhood is in no way only negative. For instance, children who are weak-minded because of birth defects remain "in paradise." They are not spiteful. They are carefree and friendly. They are happy. They do not have the possibility of developing their Adam-like understanding. But it is also impossible for them to arrive at any creative position. They are unable in their paradise to experience the freedom to choose. Similarly we see in the nature peoples, whose situation is also "paradise-like," that these peoples live without need. But they also are the peoples who remain on a primitive level of human consciousness and who cannot develop a culture for themselves.

There is also another way of staying in paradise for the individual whose parents forbid him nothing and make him completely comfortable and effortlessly snug. We notice that these children never experience the defiant stage of early development. Anxiety, lack of coordination, inability in sports because of a lack of daring, inability to relate because of unwillingness to defend oneself, are the recognizable results when the child goes to school. Later on, in extreme cases these same "children" simply do not leave home. They sit at home dry and numbed, anxious and overly conscientious in their paradise of childhood. For these individuals the maturation to full adulthood simply does not take place. Their growth is stunted, as their own moodiness and unhappiness shows. In the Bible's image language one could say: where the spirit of the snake is missing, there the spontaneous behavior of Eve cannot happen. There where the snake is missing, the beginning of self-reliance

27

and any further development are prevented by the lack of an increase in consciousness.

Seen in this way, psychopathology does not only sing us the song of the tragedy of the person who goes beyond his limits. It also reveals the positive aspects of this process. It shows us the necessity of that sting of aloneness which the isolation and the estrangement of the expulsion from paradise bring. Through these psychopathological observations we can suggest a transformation of the prohibition in Eden into a happening directed by God. That is, the development of culture and intellectual creativity described in the fall is in no way unfortunate. Rather, it is the way God begins to incarnate his spirit in humankind.

Perhaps this intentional development of human culture and spirit is what the words in Genesis refer to: "God made clothes out of skins for the man and his wife and clothed them with them." Is this an imaging of the charge to humankind to transform the animal drives within through creativity and in doing so to put new clothes on his imperfection, his nakedness?

By this the dramatic and dangerous event of the separation from God should not be understood as harmless. Nor can we say that the evil snake is simply a means of achieving a more positive goal, or that aggression ultimately effects good. No, the story of the Fall emphasizes the dangerous possibility of the corruption of persons through the spirit of the snake.

Every day, even every hour, presents us with the decision of whether to give the reins to the power drive within us. Such a decision delivers us up to the danger of falling back into the chaos of formless matter. Whoever sets himself up as the measure of all things concludes a pact with matter that finally controls all. But one cannot save oneself from this fate by killing the snake. The snake is immortal, and would in that case end up a dangerous hidden enemy. The only way to salvation from such a fate is the one in the story. There God makes clothes for humankind, thereby representing the transformation of the instinctive into good form by intentional humanness.

The story of the Fall teaches us to fear the deadly demon of our own instinct for power and control. It shows us our fate of

28

expulsion and our way into the unpredictable and continuous process of change. But the story of Jesus in the New Testament demonstrates that this bitter and painful path through change does not need to end in a fatal relationship to matter. The figure of Christ shows us that there is at the same time a model of a relationship to God which is part of the higher, more creative independence. In that figure we see our chance to receive anew the tree of eternal life through the reality of the spirit of love. This model which Christ shows us is to go bravely in the spirit of Eve through the thistles and thorns, watchfully to guard against the deadly bite of the snake, and to attend and participate in the omnipresence of God.

2.

Help for Life Through Job

Is there in our era of peace and economic well-being in the industrial world such a thing as real need? When one looks at the many well-dressed, merrily busy people on the street, it may appear that at least many of them are burdenlessly content. But the waiting list for physicians of the soul tells another story. The number of those seeking help is growing continuously.

When these needy sit down with their counselors, they most often complain: "Why does it have to be *me* who is so unlucky? Why must I suffer so? What did I do to deserve such a lot? You can see how everyone else is so happy. And many of them are not as good as I am. They are cheerful, healthy, and happy. Why is there so much injustice in the world?"

This question about the meaning of suffering and this protest against the difficulty of a seemingly undeserved fate is not unique to our time. This is one of the most burning questions of humankind of all times. Nor is ours the first time that people have turned away from religion. History has already seen that exactly as a result of some hard fate.

"What good is a pastor?" asked a patient who discovered the local minister beside her bed the day after an unsuccessful suicide attempt. "I lost my husband and both my sons in the war. Since then I don't want to have anything to do with religion. God's mercy, the power of prayer, justice—those are just empty phrases. Life is without meaning. And for me there is no way out."

These words of doubt contain a mistake. That is the conclusion that others are not in need just because their public behavior is normal. People who trust enough to speak with others of their worries discover exactly the opposite. There is practically no one who is *not* in some kind of need. Even in the lives of the so-called free spirits one can usually discover with relative ease a brittle facade whose instability threatens to produce catastrophes of even greater proportions. Their carefree attitude, upon closer inspection, resembles a dance on the edge of a sleeping volcano. Many other people of our day repress their own needs. They make the mistake of screening themselves from their needs with television or other diversions.

Such repression is costly. A person becomes dull and apathetic, and his inner development stagnates. Repression, we know since Freud, is basically no solution. It only results in making the problems even more complex, even in more need of conscious consideration. Behind the facade one discovers then the radical question: Who is without need—and how do we deal with our need?

Now, there are some needs that can be removed with relative ease. There are medications to chase pain. Operations and treatments often do eliminate certain illnesses. Certain social needs are solved simply with financial aid from the government, the church, or a private sector. It is possible to make changes in one's profession or household if the relationships therein become intolerable. Psychologist H. D. Thoreaux proposes an optimistic basis for acting when he says: "There is no life-style from which one cannot escape. Look at your own situation. If it does not please you, then change it."

Yes, there are some dead-end situations, some despondent moods that can be done away with in this way. Calling on one's own power to act can really help, but certainly not in every case.

Often it is a mistake to think that misfortune is called forth by external circumstances. Misfortune first becomes visible in the world of the external, but often these difficulties originate in one's own inner imbalances, lack of character, and conflicts. Now, perhaps in such cases it is possible to change one's character—through insight of a psychological nature or through the love of another.

But there are also cases in which that is not possible. In the same way there are incurable diseases and imperfect social conditions which even with the best abilities cannot be made right. Indeed, there are situations where there is nothing more to do. This is why even today—in spite of medicine, all kinds of technology, and every sort of social organization—we cannot escape the question: How do I deal with my own unresolvable needs? Must I lose myself in doubt and reject all belief in the positive meaning of life?

This kind of overwhelming doubt is a continual temptation for humankind. In The Book of Job the devil speaks to God about this vulnerable part of human character: "Do you think that Job would fear God otherwise? You have insured him and all that he does. You have blessed the work of his hands, and his ownership of land has expanded. But stretch out your hand and touch all that he possesses. I'm sure he will curse you to your face." And when Job is put to the test and does not fulfill the devil's prediction, the devil makes a new, more rigorous proposal: "A man will give away all he has to save his life. But stretch out your hand and lay a finger on his bone and flesh. I'm sure he will curse you to your face." This devilish voice, this temptation to turn away from trust in God, is audible every day of our era. For that reason, the story of Job and God's answer to him is extremely relevant to our situation.

Job is like many contemporary people. He remains almost entirely unshaken in his belief. When he has lost all his belongings and all his children, it is a hard blow. But he remains true to God. He says: "Naked I came from my mother's womb. Naked I will return. The Lord gives and the Lord takes away. Let the name of the Lord be praised." And even after he has been covered "from head to toe with terrible sores" and after his wife has ceased to believe in God, he speaks steadfastly: "Should we receive goodness from God and then refuse to accept the bad?"

But today, like then, the old German proverb applies: "A long stretch of time brings a burden with it." And finally after seven days and seven sleepless nights Job can no longer keep from complaining. Certainly these "seven days" are not to be taken all too realistically. The number seven mythologically always indicates a dramatic sequence reaching a climax which produces a changed situation. After seven mythological days, the complaint against God becomes more intense, more bitter, and more doubt-filled. Add to this that Job is not only suffering under this gruesome affliction. He also has to contend with his so-called friends. These are the friends who do not understand his complaint. They are of the opinion that Job's cry is not simply an all too human expression of his need. These friends think that Job has deserved the disease, that it is a deserved punishment from God, and that Job need only repent. The torment of Job is threefold, as it is with most people today, no matter whether they are in physical, material, or spiritual need. They feel deserted by God and unjustly treated, and finally they have to suffer the lack of understanding, of gloating, and the degradation of their fellow human beings. In this way their own need becomes all the more intolerable.

But this portrayal of the human situation does not fully describe the truths in the story of Job. If one considers the events with reference to the levels of subjectivity (I have described, in Chapter 1, the definition that depth psychology gives to this and its applicability to our task), Job's suffering is not to be understood as some external fate. Rather, on those levels it becomes a process originating inside us.

The power of the soul is, in such happenings, sharply reduced. The symbolic expression of this in our story is Job's loss of his possessions and his children, and his wife's loss of faith. Here all development stops, and pressure for change reaches a high point. These stages of suffering are even more burdensome through the four accusers. These accusers are of course also not only tactless friends. They represent Job's own conscience and gnawing thoughts of self-accusation. We in depth psychology observe all too often in our practice that people faced with misfortune are loaded down with guilt feelings. This sense of guilt in many cases threatens to suffocate the person completely. Such exaggerated feelings of guilt hinder and endanger the positive transformation which suffering can provoke. Job becomes a model for us by actively resisting the unreal and exaggerated guilt feelings. And the fact that at the end of the story God judges the friends shows clearly that masochistic behavior contradicts the creative urge.

That does not mean that the Bible wants to minimize the phenomenon of guilt. In other Biblical stories it is clear how humankind is guilty of grasping after power and of alienating God and others. Such guilt necessitates conversion and penance.

But here in the story of Job we recognize that there is also such a thing as a false and destructive feeling of guilt. This is a misuse of our ability to perceive our own guilt. This is an expression of a destructive desire for pain in humankind. It is impossible to see this desire as a creative force or as pleasing to God. For that reason God speaks to one of the friends: "My anger has ignited against you and your two friends, because you have not spoken the truth about me as Job has." But the most profound message which depth psychology can interpret in the story of Job lies in God's answer from the heart of the tempest. This answer contains much more than a demonstration of the wonderful nature of God. For it is this answer which allows Job to trust once more in God and to recognize that his complaint is unjust. At the end Job says: "I have spoken unwisely. I have been holding forth on matters beyond me and my knowledge. . . . But now I have seen you with my own eyes."

That is, Job obtained through God's answer the insight that made it possible to accept life without continuing to quarrel with God.

If that is possible, then it must be of burning interest to us to see how this answer looks.

The astounding thing about the answer is that this long

34

speech of God "from the tempest" is a wonderful series of pictures of creation. God's speech, upon closer examination, is in no way simply a realistic portrayal of natural processes on earth. Rather, in this imaginative interpretation of the creation it becomes a conversion to a purposeful act. The beginning of this text reads as follows:

> Where were you when I laid the earth's foundations? Tell me, since you are so well-informed! Who decided the dimensions of it, do you know? Or who stretched the measuring line across it? What supports its pillars at their bases? Who laid its cornerstone when all the stars of the morning were singing with joy and the children of God were chanting praise?

The creation of the earth is compared here to the construction of a house, whose architect and builder is God. The fact that God boasts of his creation and asserts the lack of humankind's contribution to it shifts lightly the focus of Job's question about the meaning of suffering. For a God who only answers Job's complaint with long hymns to his own supernatural power gives his creatures no hope. That would come close to Job's annihilation rather than his salvation as a result of an understanding of God's reply. Central to this part of the reply is God's assertion that the creation has something to do with cornerstones and measuredness, that there really is a definite form to existence. It is this form which limits and makes differences.

That the accent of the answer lies on this aspect of creation is immensely clear in the next verses:

> Who pent up the sea behind closed doors when it leapt tumultuous out of the womb, when I wrapped it in a robe of mist and made black clouds its swaddling bands; when I marked the bounds it was not to cross and made it fast with a bolted gate? Come thus far, I said, and no farther: here you proud waves shall break.

Creation means the taming and limiting of the sea. "Bounds" are marked and "gates" are made secure. Creation is separation and determined order, is the answer. It signifies a departure from the diffuse and unlimited nature of the beginning situation. Creation is the taming of an enormous strength, a grasping hold of the undifferentiated.

Here the text makes it clear that it is not simply speaking of the making of dry land. The text says that God made clouds into swaddling bands for the sea. This imagery shows that, just like the house in the first verses, the sea and the dry land are used as metaphors that reveal a definite content. In dreams today the sea and water are symbols for unformed and unconscious forces. Many who cannot maintain a conscious structure of their inner life dream that they are sinking into the sea, overwhelmed by the waves and on the point of being swallowed up. Those who are mentally ill and addicts also know these kinds of fantasy.

The sea is a symbol for the power of chaos, for formless unity, and for the undifferentiated nature of the beginning. The existence of creation consists of the limiting of the primeval chaos. But interestingly enough the sea is not only limited in this description of the events of creation. The sea is also darkened. The metaphor of brightness stands in the language of the soul for clarity of consciousness in contrast to the secretive, vague, "dark" areas. Creation, as it is understood here, signifies the strengthening of the conscious. In the pictures of the next verse this recognition is empowered through the use of additional symbols:

> Have you ever in your life given orders to the morning or sent the dawn to its post, telling it to grasp the earth by its edges and shake the godless out of it? I change the earth to sealing clay and dye it as a man dyes clothes; stealing the light from the godless and breaking the arm ready to strike.

This is even more clearly parabolic language. It is impossible to see it simply as a description of the natural event of dawn. God's creation is *like* the morning, it is *like* a stamped seal. This signified the process of consciousness, the "enlightening." The work of this God produces "stealing the light from the godless and breaking the arm ready to strike." Creation means therefore also the possibility of deciding between good and bad. It represents not only limit but also judgment.

Here we see clearly that creation is understood as a model of spiritual formation, and not simply as an external process. The text knows that it is also describing an inner happening which has to do with being able to order and make judgments about life. Such an ability is not always possible in humankind, however, since humankind is itself a part of creation and does not always have the dark primeval powers in its consciousness. The following verses speak of this difficulty of humankind:

> Have you journeyed all the way to the depths of the sea, or walked where the Abyss is deepest? Have you been shown the gates of Death or encountered the gates of Shadowland? Have you an inkling of the extent of the earth? Tell me about it if you have. Which is the way to the home of the light, and where does darkness live? You could show them the way to their proper places, or put them on the path to where they live. If you know all this, you must have been born with them, you must be very old by now.

Again we should not understand "light" and "darkness" only as the difference between night and day. Rather, this is a reference to the difference between order and chaos, good and evil, the enlightenment of the conscious and the darkness of the unconscious, form and formlessness. The words, "you must have been born with them," are, however, an assertion that the creation—yes, the birth of each individual human being—signifies a new formation and consciousness which limits the "darkness."

But even as the human being can reach so little of the depth dimension and the primeval chaos with his consciousness, so also is it extremely difficult for him to perceive clearly the laws of the spirit. The workings of the spirit are often portrayed in mythological language in images of wind, rain, dew, hail, and snow, because they come "from above." Human beings see the spirit psychically as "above" and the material as "below."

Concerning the ancient Jewish symbolism of these natural

"Which is the way to the home of the light, and where does
darkness live?"

events, Friedrich Weinreb writes: "Always when there is talk of rain or some other natural happening, one knows that it is a consideration of things which are present in an absolute sense. Such occurrences represent the deepest kind of identity. Of rain one knows that it exists as a phenomenon in our world because the heavens give people the possibility of fruitfulness and growth. In other words, the rain shows us the dependence of the earthly on the heavenly world." Similarly hail comes as punishment or testing of humans. And like the impenetrable storm, God shows himself effective. His spirit, it is said, replenishes and destroys, it transforms and renews:

> Have you ever visited the place where the ice is kept, or seen where the hail is stored up, which I keep for times of stress, for days of battle and war? From which direction does the lightning fork when it scatters sparks over the earth? Who carves a channel for the downpour, and hacks a way for the rolling thunder, so that the rain may fall on lands where no one lives, and the deserts void of human dwelling, giving drink to the lonely wastes and making grass spring where everything was dry? Has the rain a father? Who begets the dewdrops? What womb brings forth the ice, and gives birth to the heaven, when the waters are hidden and the surface of the deep freezes?

The laws of the spirit are alien and impenetrable to humankind. They are as uncontrollable as the order of the stars or the weather in Job's day.

> Can you fasten the harness of the Seven Stars, or untie Orion's bands? Can you guide the morning star season by season and show the Bear and its cubs which way to go? Have you grasped the celestial laws? Could you make their writ run on the earth? Can your voice carry as far as the clouds and make the pent-up waters do your bidding? Will lightning flashes come at your command and answer, "Here we are"? Who gives wisdom in the midst of the hidden? Who gives understandable thoughts? Whose skill details every cloud and tilts the flasks of heaven until the soil cakes into a solid mass and clods of earth cohere together?

But these clarifications of the nature of the creation do not make up the substance of God's "answer." They serve only as an introduction. On the one hand they accent Job's inability to make judgments and therefore the unjustified nature of his complaint. On the other hand they tell us something about the power of creation, that it is essentially an opponent of chaos. In creation, chaos is not done away with, it is only banished. Meaning for living creatures consists in the perpetual and increasing banishing of the formless, of the dead matter. In this way every person can become God's servant. In fact, every person is that servant of God inasmuch as he or she is a formed being. Therefore the "meaning of life" is already fulfilled, if we make it through this life without despairing, without "cursing God." For in this way our life is a grain of sand in God's dike against nothingness. On this level every life which struggles toward form becomes a special contribution and a necessary strengthening of God's will.

For instance, a person who thinks herself "only a housewife," who manages for decades to be undaunted and patient, is, according to our text, a much more worthy "handmaid of the Lord" than some adored artist who drags his fellow human beings through his own despondency. Works of this kind are perversions of the real essence of artistic creativity. Such "tempters" deliver one into the hands of chaos instead of leading one away from chaos with artistic talents.

The question of the meaning of suffering is much more directly answered in the following chapters of Job. In these chapters there is a dominance of symbolic animals. That the text is not simply describing the animal world is evident in the following verse:

Who makes provision for the raven when his squabs cry out to God and fly confusedly around, because they have nothing to eat?

Objectively this description of the birds' behavior is not correct and contradicts the most elementary observations. Young ravens do not fly confusedly around because they do not have anything to eat. They starve in the nest if the parents do not come again to feed them. This difficulty is removed if one understands that the raven is a mythological symbol for spiritual wisdom. God's spirit is communicated to people through certain wise persons. These persons bring the "food," that is, the recognition of God's spirit, to the "young squabs" (the spiritually immature people). How does this food look which verse 41 refers to? It contains the recognition that creation on the one hand is clear and lively form with definite boundaries and that on the other hand creation leaves her creatures free. In freedom lies their potential and their danger. For being left free means being confronted with the powers of darkness. Suffering is a result of such battles and as such always a test, just as Satan said at the beginning of the story. Suffering is then a temptation and a testing which God cannot keep from humankind. For God needs people as his fellow workers in creation. If creation is understood as an ongoing consciousness-raising and decision-making process inside the person, then in each life the spirit must continually wrestle successfully with the powers of chaos.

Creation is not simply a past accomplishment of God's. It is just as much the continual triumph of the spirit over chaos and formless matter in humankind itself. This process can only complete itself in confrontation with the darkness. For this reason people must be tested in their role as the essential landmark of the incarnation of God's spirit in matter. For that reason Job is tested. For that reason God says at the beginning to Satan:

> "Did you notice my servant Job? There is no one like him on the earth: a sound and honest man who fears God and shuns evil." "Yes," Satan said, "but Job is not God-fearing for nothing, is he? You have blessed all he undertakes, and his flocks throng the countryside. But stretch out your hand and lay a finger on his possessions: I guarantee you, he will curse you to your face." "Very well," the Lord said to Satan, "all he has is in your power."

The assumption that people who are like Job can be servants of God is due to their being left free. For that reason the following verses sing of the freedom of God's creatures. In this way God compares the process of creation to the process of the birth of goats and hinds. Right in the first picture the text says:

> They crouch to drop their young, and let their burdens fall, and they leave them, never to return.

And then:

> Who gave the wild donkey his freedom, and untied the rope from his proud neck?

After that the wild donkey becomes the symbol of the spiritually free person, who resists temptation and strives for the spiritual "heights."

> He scorns the turmoil of the city: there are no shouts from a driver for him to listen for. The mountains are the pastures that he seeks in quest of green blade or leaf.

The desert, the turmoil of the city, and the shouts of the driver stand in this case for the "unfruitful," meaningless activities of the world. People who are like wild donkeys look for higher levels. These higher levels are represented by the image of the mountains.

A variation on this freedom of the creature appears in the picture of the wild ox:

> Is the wild ox willing to serve you or spend a night beside your manger? If you tie a rope round his neck, will he harrow the furrows for you? Can you rely on his massive strength and leave him to do your heavy work? Can you depend on him to come home carrying your grain to your threshing floor?

The wild ox is often used in mythology as a symbol for the phallic-creative spirit. But this spirit is also completely free. One cannot assume that people in whom the wild ox's spirit comes to life (for instance, artists) will use it in the service of creation.

42

Nor is it certain that they will bring their life's work (their seed) to the Lord's barn.

The spirit of God is symbolized in the Holy Scriptures, as in mythology, by a winged animal or bird. In Job we see the stork, the falcon, and the eagle. The eagle is described as follows:

> She lives in the cliffs and spends her nights among the crags and on the unclimbed peaks.

How much the text is concentrating on the process of becoming spiritually free is expressed especially in the symbol of the ostrich egg. Mythologically the large egg is a symbol for a process of becoming before it begins. It is a symbol of hope for a spiritually fulfilled life. Here the text speaks of the ostrich like this:

> She leaves her eggs on the ground with only earth to warm them; forgetting that a foot may tread on them or a wild beast may crush them. Cruel to her chicks as if they were not hers, little she cares if her labor goes for nothing. God, you see, has made her unwise, and given her no share of common sense. Yet if she bestirs herself to use her height, she can make fools of horse and man too.

The making real of the spirit (the opening of the eggs) takes place in matter (in the unfertile desert sand). In this way the spirit is practically turned over to nature, as Job is turned over to Satan. Yes, the spirit can be destroyed (the eggs can be stepped on, the wild animals can crush them). That is, persons can be so overwhelmed by the superior force of their sickness, their physical needs, their drives, and the power of matter that the divine spirit in them dies. For people are like the ostrich, the text says. They are not insightful. They cannot distinguish between the essential and the nonessential. For that reason, we read: "God has made her unwise, and given her no share of common sense."

But then at the same time the text states that this need not be the case. The divine spirit in humankind can be victorious. A kind of power can unfold which exceeds the speed of a runner or a horse. As we read: "Yet if she bestirs herself to use her height, she can make fools of horse and man too."

The positive spirit of opposition and steadfastness is portrayed with the image of a war-horse. This is a spirit in the person which makes it possible to stand up to the battles of life and to encounter the challenges of evil (here "chiefs"):

> Are you the one who makes the horse so brave and covers his neck with flowing hair? Do you make him leap like a grasshopper? His proud neighing spreads terror far and wide. Exultantly he paws the soil of the valley, and prances eagerly to meet the clash of arms. He laughs at fear; he is afraid of nothing, he recoils before no sword. On his back the quiver rattles, the flashing spear and javelin. Quivering with impatience, he eats up the miles; when the trumpet sounds, there is no holding him. At each trumpet blast he shouts "Hurrah!" He scents the battle from afar, hearing the thundering of chiefs, the shouting.

The meaning of life lies in the battle and work for God and his creation. This is unintimidated steadfastness. It is decisiveness against the undecided, formation against blurred chaos. This is not the place for complaint. This is where we are called to awareness with which we engage "pride" and "godlessness" (Job 40:11,12). Here also is where God tells us, "Your own right hand can assure your triumph" (Job 40:14). The right hand, a symbol of energy and of healthy human insight, makes it easier to complete the right decisions. Without insight and energy this crucial capacity to make judgments does not belong to humankind.

In view of this situation God now conveys a further insight about his creation to Job. This time God introduces the monsters Behemoth and Leviathan:

> Now think of Behemoth; he eats greenstuff like the ox. But what strength he has in his loins, what power in his stomach muscles! His tail is as stiff as a cedar, the sinews of his thighs are tightly knit. His vertebrae are bronze tubing, his bones as hard as hammered iron. He is the beginning of God's way, but his Maker threatened him with the sword, forbidding him the mountain regions where

all the wild beasts have their playground. So he lies beneath the lotus, and hides among the reeds in the swamps. The leaves of the lotus give him shade, the willows by the stream shelter him. Should the river overflow on him, why should he worry? A Jordan could pour down his throat without his caring. So who is going to catch him by the eyes or drive a peg through his nostrils?

Behemoth, the symbol of sexuality and the drive for nourishment, is more primeval than dangerous. "He eats greenstuff like the ox. But what strength he has in his loins." He is the anticipation of the incarnation of the divine spirit, since the text reads: "He is the beginning of God's way." The danger to the person from Behemoth lies in the inertia of this natural phenomenon when it becomes dominant. Behemoth can devour the strength of a person. He can swallow the living stream that nourishes a person, just as he could take in the whole Jordan river. For that reason the text reads: "The leaves of the lotus give him shade, the willows by the stream shelter him. Should the river overflow on him, why should he worry?" This powerful and primeval instinct does not let itself be overwhelmed. It does not let someone lead it around with a ring in its nose. This tremendous insight of the Old Testament has not really been taken to heart in the history of the church. Only in recent times have we realized that this instinctive power within persons is not repressible. If repressed, it reappears in the form of uncontrolled mental illness. Instead of repression or mental illness there is now another alternative for humankind in relationship with Behemoth. Now there is the possibility of knowing and respecting one's own drives. This entails a good deal of recognition of one's own powerlessness. Respect for one's own drives stands over against both repression and manipulation. For today's society also knows about the manipulations of these drives through fashion fads and sex in advertising.

But Job receives his most direct answer to his question about his need in the description of Leviathan. The battle of God against the monster Leviathan is an archetypal myth. It resembles the battle of the heroes against the dragon, a story that is much older than the Holy Scriptures. It carries a similar message to God's taming of the sea. It is a symbol for the original creative act, the empowering of matter through form and order. This monster is also "made good," but it stands in opposition to God. The freedom of the whole creation necessitates that humankind live side by side with Leviathan without possessing the power to conquer him. Leviathan is a symbol for matter-dominated nature of the most merciless kind in and around us.

> Leviathan, too! Can you catch him with a fish-hook or run a line round his tongue? Can you put a ring through his nose or pierce his jaw with a hook? Will he plead and plead with you, will he coax you with smooth words? Will he strike a bargain with you to become your slave for life? Will you make a pet of him, like a bird, keep him on a lead to amuse your maids? Is he to be sold by the fishing guild and then retailed by merchants? Riddle his hide with darts? Prod his head with a harpoon? You have only to lay a finger on him never to forget the struggle or risk it again! Any hopes you might have would prove vain, for the mere sight of him would stagger you.

This Leviathan is the devouring and destructive aspect of nature, the symbol of aggression, of evil, and of the power of evil.

> Who dare open the gates of his mouth? Terror dwells in those rows of teeth!

But this power also has a definite shape. In Leviathan an order dominates, which is portrayed in the image of the scales. Like the causal laws in nature, the scales on Leviathan's back stick together.

> His scales are like a row of shields, sealed with a seal of stone, touching each other so close that not a breath could pass between; sticking to one another to make an indivisible whole.

And the gruesome, inexorable hardness of nature is portrayed in these words:

His heart is as hard as rock, and fear itself flees from him.

The horrors of nature like natural catastrophes, anger, hate, revenge, and murder are described as Leviathan's breath of fire and sharp fragments sticking from his body:

> From his mouth come fiery torches, sparks of fire fly out of it. His nostrils belch smoke like a cauldron boiling on the fire. His breath could kindle coals, so hot a flame issues from his mouth. . . . He has sharp potsherds underneath, and moves across the slime like a harrow. He churns the depths into a seething cauldron, he makes the sea fume like a scent burner. Behind him he leaves a glittering wake—a white fleece seems to float on the deeps. He has no equal on earth, being created without fear. He looks the haughtiest in the eye; of all the sons of pride he is the king.

Thus God finished his speech.

Yes, people are subject to these powers. We experience them in the conditions of incurable sickness or in confrontation with degenerations in character such as artifice, sadism, lust for power, and violence. We know them also in ourselves, in our own anger and in other "fiery" feelings. And they assault us too through war or an airplane crash or in a natural catastrophe.

People in this kind of need require the knowledge that in the Old Testament there is explanation. In The Book of Job, God justifies himself in the eyes of the persons who want to lay claim to freedom through life and therefore freedom through the dark and seemingly destructive experiences. For God has conquered Leviathan. Nevertheless Leviathan lives, like Satan, in creation. And he can, as Satan did to Job, catapult human beings into terrible suffering. It is inadequate to fight against Leviathan with technical means (with spears, lances, or swords).

> Sword may strike him, but cannot pierce him; no more can spear, javelin, or lance. Iron means no more to him than straw, nor bronze than rotten wood. The arrow does not make him run, sling stones he treats as wisps of hay. A club strikes him like a reed, he laughs at the whirring javelin.

What arrogance it is to think that these powers in and around us could be defeated with spears. These means are finally doomed to failure, like, for instance, the battle of the physician against death. All that is material is finally submitted to death. Leviathan is unconquerable. Every human attempt to win a victory through technical means over the deadly power of matter is finally insufficient. Only humility and the "right hand," which the "arrogant" and the "godless" condemn, can help against Behemoth and Leviathan. The "right hand" is the healthy human insight and the winged spirit which, like the eagle, peers beyond the earthly. This is the spirit which suspects that God has more for him than to deliver him over to the power of nature and the material death.

The existence of evil in the world, as suffering and need remind us, is unavoidable. But each proof of faithfulness to God and to the spirit of order has meaning. It is an invasion into the territory of evil and as such the perfection and completion of more "creation." If we regard the suffering of humankind in this way, we suddenly see that heavy and undeserved misfortune is not merely a testing. It even can be an honor. It can be the fulfillment of God's hope of finding in his "servant" Job a tree that resists the stormy shock of Leviathan and that in doing so furthers creation itself.

Seen in this way, a patiently endured yet inscrutable sickness or a lack of bitterness in a person crippled by an automobile accident contain a sacred consecration of life itself. When a person stands the test of suffering and draws the same conclusion as Job drew, he goes forth purified by such a trial by fire. Then—so the end of Job's story tells us—that person is blessed with productivity and richness. Of course, this image does not mean material wealth or many children. Faithfulness to God and completion of his creation result in the disappearance of anxiety about life and death. This co-creation with God takes the punch out of the bitterness in suffering and the questions about the justice of it all.

For suffering in this life, the suffering which Leviathan prepares for us, carries with it the chance to transform and purify beings. Through trust in God and in the purposefulness of his

48

Faithfulness to God and completion of his creation result in the disappearance of anxiety about life and death

creation the acceptance and enduring of need becomes possible because it is transformed into a meaning-oriented test and an accomplishment *for God*. To stumble into need, to find oneself surrounded by meaninglessness, signifies living through forgiveness. In such cases the "sea of chaos" swallows one up. Inasmuch as we live, we have decided for the Creator-God, the former of our being. The only questions are whether we can confirm this decision in the unavoidable suffering of life and whether we remain true to ourselves. In doing so, we are true to God. In the bearing of suffering is hidden a promise, which is expressed explicitly in The Book of Enoch: "The darkness is abolished. There will be unceasing light. Leviathan is divided and eaten up." (Enoch 58:6.) Need, despair, and new hope (spiritual death and renewal) are the requirements for a gradual embodiment of the natural powers in an all-embracing spiritual power.

The images in God's speech from the heart of the tempest can show us today how the divine value system is to be understood. In those images we discover that creation is the fundamental value for God. So there is a divine preference of initiative over inertia, of spirit over matter, and of the struggle to give form and to decide over an undifferentiated pluralism.

In the figure of Christ the New Testament makes available a concrete confirmation of this value system. Our goal, the overcoming of chaos, is nearer through him. For Christ it is the spirit of love which is the primary weapon against Leviathan. Because of that love principle the final answer of Christ to Job is: "I am the truth and the life. Whoever believes in me will have eternal life, even though he die." The steadfastness of life in the midst of suffering is guaranteed by *love*. This assurance leads through discipleship of Christ to the triumphant shout of Paul: "Death is swallowed up in victory. Death, where is your sting? Hell, where is your victory?" (I Cor. 15:55.) The Bible's answer to the cry of existential need is not one of external change or pragmatic strategizing. No, the Bible paints a picture of promise. It is a challenging picture of inner transformation through suffering.

50

3.

The Timeless Truth of the Jonah Story

A doctor called me to the hospital. He had there, he said, a young patient who had just almost killed himself with an overdose. Apparently the young man was not addicted. He had no withdrawal symptoms. He was struggling against the domination of his parents. Finally he fled to a commune, for which, however, he appeared to possess no affection. In any case, no one from there had responded to his situation. The doctor said the patient was very depressed and would hardly accept food. He was simply lying in his bed apathetically and would barely respond at all when addressed.

When I saw this twenty-one-year-old patient for the first time, I immediately had the impression that he had already experienced the worst of his depression. He looked at me with clear eyes, smiled, and said, "I think I'm on land again." I ventured the response, "When one has been so far under, that is a great feeling, isn't it?"

"Yes," he said. "You know, I was like a stone which some-one had thrown into the ocean. I fell and fell and fell, and was so heavy and completely powerless. It was as if a huge and monstrous mouth had swallowed me and completely cut off any chance for me ever to escape. Somehow, I don't know when, things got better. I dreamed about home, and our family business, which I direct. And when I awoke, I knew at once that everything had gone wrong and that I really messed things up. I had shirked my duty. I had been cowardly, and had simply walked away from all I should have done—but had nevertheless thought of myself as a kind of hero. I'm sure you want to know what I mean by that. My father owns a pretty big business in which I have been quite involved. I was always interested in the work. My father is not at all authoritarian. Naturally he said he would be happy if I would succeed him. But he also said that I should decide what to study. Things could always be managed without me, if I didn't want to choose this business, he said.

"Somehow I felt that wasn't the case. There were a number of things I didn't like about the business. Often it was just the suitableness of his choice which bothered me. And the weekly magazine he puts out is nothing more than sleepy drivel. There would be a lot to change to get our materialistic generation on the right track. You can count on everything going wrong if people sleep on and continue to think only of their own things. When I talked about that, my father only laughed. 'You can only make judgments like that when you have been around long enough,' he would say. Well, then, I thought, I should just dive in. But then I began to feel inferior and think that everyone knew better than I and that they really didn't want me. And all at once I got the feeling that if they didn't need me here, no one needs me. At that point I ran away. I left school and home. After a while, when my money was all gone, I got involved in the commune. The people there had also given up their bourgeois life and worked off and on. The bad part of it was that I became more depressed. I didn't get up in the morning. I didn't work, and just let myself be led by the others. In our community that was often the reason for big fights. A lot of the people were just lying around. One time we had a huge blowup. Everybody was screaming. A couple of them were hitting each other. Chairs were broken. And then they all said that I was to blame. They said I ruined their community. And they literally kicked me out of the house. There I was, sitting on the doorstep. What a plight! I couldn't understand it at all. Then and there I took the drugs that I had on me. I tripped out. Before then I had just hustled drugs for the others. The next thing I knew, I was here in the hospital."

There wasn't really much need for therapy after that. The young man had already realized that he had fled from an impulse inside himself. He saw clearly that all the resources he needed to work for social change in the world were available to him by taking over the position in the company. He proceeded to return to that position and consciously set about his task of inner and outer transformation.

While noting that this young man did not understand altogether what duty he had fled and exactly how he had been cured, we can point out that his story is simply a new edition of the old story of Jonah, who sought to flee from his duty. Here is the Biblical version of that story:

The word of Yahweh was addressed to Jonah son of Amittai: "Up!" he said. "Go to Nineveh, the great city, and inform them that their wickedness has become known to me." Jonah decided to run away from Yahweh, and to go to Tarshish. He went down to Joppa and found a ship bound for Tarshish; he paid his fare and went aboard, to go with them to Tarshish, to get away from Yahweh. But Yahweh unleashed a violent wind on the sea, and there was such a great storm at sea that the ship threatened to break up. The sailors took fright, and each of them called on his own god, and to lighten the ship they threw the cargo overboard. Jonah, however, had gone below and lain down in the hold and fallen fast asleep. The boatswain came upon him and said, "What do you mean by sleeping? Get up! Call upon your god! Perhaps he will spare us and not leave us to die." Then they said to each other, "Come on, let us draw lots to find out who is responsible for bringing this evil on us." So they cast lots, and the lot fell to Jonah. Then they said to him, "Tell us, what is your business? Where do you come from? What is your country? What is your nationality?" He replied, "I am a Hebrew, and I worship Yahweh, the God of heaven, who made the sea and the land." The sailors were seized with terror at this and said, "What have you done?" They knew that he was trying to escape from Yahweh, because he had told them so. They then said, "What are we to do with you, to make the sea grow calm for us?" For the sea was growing rougher and rougher. He replied, "Take me and throw me into the sea, and then it will grow calm for you. For I can see it is my fault this violent storm has happened to you." The sailors rowed hard in an effort to reach the shore, but in vain, since the sea grew rougher still for them. They called on Yahweh and said, "O Yahweh, do not let us perish for taking this man's life; do not hold us guilty of innocent blood; for you, Yahweh, have acted as you have thought right." And taking hold of Jonah they threw him into the sea; and the sea grew calm again. At this the men were seized with dread of Yahweh; they offered a sacrifice to Yahweh and made vows.

Yahweh had arranged that a great fish should be there to swallow Jonah; and Jonah remained in the belly of the fish for three days and three nights. From the belly of the fish he prayed to Yahweh, his God, and said: "Out of my distress I cried to Yahweh and he answered me; from the belly of Sheol I cried, and you have heard my voice. You cast me into the abyss, into the heart of the sea, and the flood surrounded me. All your waves, your billows, washed over me. And I said: I am cast out from your sight. How shall I ever look again on your holy Temple? The waters surrounded me right to my throat, the abyss was all around me. The seaweed was wrapped around my head at the roots of the mountains. I went down into the countries underneath the earth, to the peoples of the past. But you lifted my life from the pit, Yahweh my God. While my soul was fainting within me, I remembered Yahweh, and my prayer came before you into your holy Temple. Those who serve worthless idols forfeit the grace that was theirs. But I, with a song of praise, will sacrifice to you. The vow I have made, I will fulfill. Salvation comes from Yahweh." Yahweh spoke to the fish, which then vomited Jonah onto the shore. The word of Yahweh was addressed a second time to Jonah: "Up!" he said. "Go to Nineveh, the great city, and preach to them as I told you to." Jonah set out and went to Nineveh in obedience to the word of Yahweh.

Jonah too had a duty. It was a duty in the world, for which the city of Nineveh is a symbol here. By preaching, he is commanded to prevent humankind from falling away from God. Just as the young man did, Jonah draws back because he basically thinks that it can happen without him. Jonah does not accept the task, first of all, because he does not take himself seriously enough. Secondly, he is afraid that people will ridicule him if he does not succeed.

But let us notice how seriously Yahweh takes Jonah. Yahweh's compassion for Nineveh in the end is not because he is arbitrarily patient and easygoing. It is precisely because Jonah preached and the people of Nineveh responded by repenting. The story of Jonah shows us how absolutely necessary human beings are for God. For that reason we run up a dead-end street if we do not take our actions seriously or do not accept our own perceptions of what needs to be done. A darkness of the soul comes over us when we attempt to flee our assigned tasks.

And is our struggle so very different ·from Jonah's boat trip? Our environment often has a kind of unconscious sense of what endangers it, and therefore seeks to push that something away and out of reach. It is only through this increasing crisis that we, the disobedient, perceive the possibility of repentance. This does not always need to come in a commune, as it did in the case of this young man. We can also be pushed out by our colleagues at work because we are carping or untrustworthy. We can be catapulted out of our families by some great "storm." All this for one purpose—that we finally begin to reflect on our situation, once we have been isolated. And once isolated, we can recognize that we have chosen to flee into a soft life instead of heeding our inner calling.

Now we can also understand the images in the story (Jonah in the bottom of the ship and his being swallowed by the great fish) as grandiose pictures of a condition of the soul. Yes, this portrays the following human situation with keenness: Many people retreat into a kind of prenatal condition, in which their depression prevents them from doing anything. The youth I encountered in the hospital illustrates this Jonah-like stance without consciously recalling it from church or school studies. He said he felt "as if a huge and monstrous mouth had swallowed" him. Such depression is really a process of being captured again by a chaotic unconsciousness. Once in this state our patients are no longer capable of developing their own activity. They lose interest in keeping themselves clean or even in keeping themselves alive. Chaos owns them again. Such a relapse is pictured perfectly in the sea and the fish's mouth which swallows Jonah. Similar images occur today in the dreams and fantasies of our contemporaries when they find themselves in such a psychic state. The images are typical expressions of human need. For that reason the story of Jonah is a timeless and transforming truth.

In the isolation of his bed at the hospital our young man suddenly understands clearly where he belongs. He even recognizes this in picture language when he says that he is "on land again." The Biblical story corresponds of course almost exactly, when it says that the fish "vomited Jonah onto the shore." The depression disappears with one blow. It comes through insight and conversion in the dark night of no exit. It is possible for a person to orient himself again and to come out of the swimming feeling of helplessness. This is the message of the image of Jonah once more having ground under his feet. Interestingly enough it is exactly the land which awaits him. The journey through the night (the process of being swallowed up by darkness) has been consistently portraying the transformation of the soul, of the soul's journey through hell, and the soul's rebirth. But the story of Jonah does not only speak of the terrible difficulties of such experiences. It characterizes these experiences as necessary parts of the process of rescue and personal change. For Jonah, who fled God, succeeded in finding him, praying to him, and obeying him precisely in his hour of need.

We who work in psychology know about another kind of journey through darkness. This is the kind that does not end on the shores of Nineveh in the morning sun. Here all doors become closed to the light. Night lasts forever as suicide confirms the misfortune.

Nineveh still exists. It is more than necessary for us to listen to determine our own calling in relationship to this city.

But this recognition is not the end of the story of Jonah. There is a second and equally meaningful part.

56

Now Nineveh was a city great beyond compare; it took three days to cross it. Jonah went on into the city, making a day's journey. He preached in these words, "Only forty days more and Nineveh is going to be destroyed." And the people of Nineveh believed in God; they proclaimed a fast and put on sackcloth, from the greatest to the least. The news reached the king of Nineveh, who rose from his throne, took off his robe, put on sackcloth and sat down in ashes. A proclamation was then promulgated throughout Nineveh by decree of the king and his ministers, as follows: "Men and beasts, herds and flocks, are to taste nothing; they must not eat, they must not drink water. All are to put on sackcloth and call on God with all their might; and let everyone renounce his evil behavior and the wicked things he has done. Who knows if God will not change his mind and relent, if he will not renounce his burning wrath, so that we do not perish?" God saw their efforts to renounce their evil behavior. And God relented: he did not inflict on them the disaster which he had threatened.

Nineveh was certainly not the only city during Jonah's time that was ready to be destroyed by its own corruption. God took pity on her because her people repented. This story can also help us to orient ourselves today. And the orientation is toward repentance. Repentance has become unfashionable today. It is uncomfortable. And our friendly pastors have become so aware of their own inabilities that they are no longer able to preach anything. They are afraid of saying anything that might appear to cause people to fear God's punishment. Theologically they maintain that the repentance of the Old Testament prophets stems from a primitive picture of God. Repentance is hardly necessary *after* Jesus Christ, they say, since God has forgiven sinners in Christ.

This is, on a number of levels, a superficial interpretation. First of all, it ignores the daily tragedies of carelessness and selfishness which we complete each day. But also it does not do the New Testament itself justice. Most clearly in the Revelation to John we read that a general absolution is not the point of Christ's coming. Indeed, destruction and damnation are threatened for the people who are arrogantly unfaithful to their creator. And is not precisely this an important point for us today? Are there not today numerous signs of need which signal the necessity of repentance?

In our culture the problem is not hunger or war. This itself is surprising, when we realize that most of the human race is undernourished. But I am referring to the problems which our Western families experience in the raising of our youth. These difficulties are growing, not decreasing. Today's difficulties are much different from before. They are penetrating and pervasive. They are not only a little insubordination here and a little laziness there and again here a little spoiledness. No, the extent of the problems makes parents beside themselves today. It results even in parental depression, when the children demonstrate that all the parental effort was for nothing. We live in a society full of addicted youth, children who vow never to see their parents again, parents and children fighting one another in court, and parents campaigning against disorder and carelessness. Some adults are punished year after year with a complete disruption of contact. This in turn results often in alcoholism or bitterness of another kind. Others are robbed of much of their possessions through the appetite of their offspring.

Recently in my practice I have encountered the following: a youth who broke into the coin collection of the parents and stole its contents, another who set the kitchen on fire, and a third who threw his lame mother off a chair and broke her arm (because she had taken his cognac bottle away). A girl from a very respected household held sexual orgies while her parents were away. Yes, I can sing a song about the suffering of many people which I have learned about in my practice. Parents of very young children who do not yet go to school are industrious and orderly and think that such things could never happen in their families. They think they will be free of these problems because they have provided themselves with an orderly garden, a house, and a car. In avoiding the apartment houses, they think they have avoided the problems in the development of their children's souls. But that has proved to be an illusion. Affluence does not protect people against neurotic neglect or drug addiction or suicide. On the contrary, statistics show that most suicides occur in comfortable or rich homes. The need of our day is not a "class problem," as the neo-Marxist would have it. Nor is it primarily a social problem which will be solved by a redistribution of the wealth. We have already seen that people do not live by bread alone. For that reason we are called to repent and do penance. The children who steal are starving in their souls. They steal without knowing why they do it. They take candy from the store in their search for the sweet love they did not find in their parents, who were so busy with their own professions. The psychic and spiritual result of living in a household where the heads are devoted primarily to earning money is disastrous. It is the child's soul which suffers. We must, of course, make some distinctions. It is justified and natural to assure one's family of food and shelter by earning money. But the child's development is hindered when all other needs are respected less than the need to be materially well-off. This worshiping of material wealth is in no way simply a result of industry's bosses. It is also [in Germany] partly due to the misuse of industry by Hitler, and the hard economic times during and after the war. Today our youth lack examples of persons who transcend their own personal needs. For it is during late adolescence, between seventeen and twenty-one years of age, that the developmental stage of societal relationships occurs. At this age the youth need to develop a more than individual purpose. They need to learn to commit themselves to events beyond themselves. Today's adults do not seem able to provide the youth with a model or even direction. And so the youth react with increasing undirected aggression, in protests, unrest, and depression.

The idolization of materialism produces even worse problems for the psychic and spiritual development of the younger children. Today they are flooded with toys and treats. This excess lames their imagination and gives them a false picture of the world. A strange impression grows within them that the roasted dove they just ate somehow flew into their mouths. When they discover a few years later that such things do not happen, they rebel and resist work. The most serious result is that through this spoiling there is a general loss of ability to act. The children enjoy activity less. There is a general atrophy of

59

activity, as I have stated in my other books. That is, a fundamental passivity develops. The bad part of it is that the children lose their best opportunity for a fulfilling life by atrophying during this early stage. This emptiness also seems to be accompanied by a real unhappiness.

I believe that the significance of this awesome need which countless parents and children experience today is its warning to us. It warns us to combat this danger as soon as possible. It calls us to recognize that the human being as individual person and collective phenomenon will be destroyed, if materialism (whether liberal or dialectic) becomes our God. Humanity will either regress into the dictatorship of a socialistic pseudo paradise or will sink into the chaos of material affluence, unless materialism is rejected.

Salvation for our Nineveh can come neither from the false prophets of the east nor the west. We need most of all to do what the people of Nineveh did—they believed God, our text says. That is the absolutely crucial step. That should and must be the conclusion we draw from our dilemma. How selfish it is to think that a child can grow up without the love of its mother! How arrogant to think that one need only send a child to a sitter while the mother goes to work. How strange it is to ignore the essential value of a mother's love and sacrifice for a child's development. And how clearly we see Christ's words illustrated: You cannot serve two masters—God and mammon. Certainly we must support ourselves materially. But that cannot become our primary objective in life. Above all, we must value obedience, respect, love, and service for God. Love for one's neighbor and love for the children become primary goals.

It is not easy. It requires enormous effort to change our materialist, egocentric, spoiled, and comfortable attitude. It is better for our children that we spend time with them than that we earn enough to purchase them a new toy every day. It is better for the children in the early school years when we camp and play with them than when we charge around in a new automobile. It is better to play with them than to spend time and money for new clothing outfits for them. It is immeasurably better to keep the infants on our own breasts for three fourths of a year than to spoil them with a ready-made and unnatural form of nourishment.

This need for a conscious abstinence from the comforts of our society helps us understand the text's emphasis on fasting. It becomes the image for the curing of our sick dependency on the culture of consumption. But we too, like Nineveh, need the model of our "king" or "chief," the guiding force of the soul to bend the knees in ashes. Penance for the soul needs to replace self-congratulatory throne-sitting. The following image of the animals who are not even allowed to eat during the time of penance fills out our text's description of the penitential act. A change in direction, repentance, occurs through a temporary halt of nourishment to the "primitive, bestial" drives in us. The gods of desire and consumption and spoiling and money are false gods. Their falseness is demonstrated by the picture we have just painted of the future of the current generation. If we want to have a genuine future and not be buried by the anger of God, we should all, like the people of Nineveh, call for a great fast. This means a change in our attitude. It means embracing a fear of God, a love for human beings, and a readiness to commit and sacrifice.

The last part of the Jonah story accents something other than what we have been discussing. Jonah experiences that his prophecy of Nineveh's destruction does not come true. His response is one of displeasure.

Jonah was very indignant at this; he fell into a rage. He prayed Yahweh and said, "Ah! Yahweh, is not this just as I said would happen when I was still at home? That was why I went and fled to Tarshish: I knew that you were a God of tenderness and compassion, slow to anger, rich in graciousness, relenting from evil. So now, Yahweh, please take my life away, for I might as well be dead as go on living." Yahweh replied, "Are you right to be angry?" Jonah then went out of the city and sat down to the east of the city. There he made himself a shelter and sat under it in the shade, to see what would happen to the city. Then Yahweh God arranged that a castor oil plant should grow up over Jonah to give shade for his head and soothe his ill-humor; Jonah was delighted with the castor oil plant. But at dawn the next day, God arranged that a worm should attack the castor oil plant—and it withered. Next, when the sun rose, God arranged that there should be a scorching east wind; the sun beat down so hard on Jonah's head that he was overcome and begged for death, saying, "I might as well be dead as go on living." God said to Jonah, "Are you right to be angry about the castor oil plant?" He replied, "I have every right to be angry, to the point of death." Yahweh replied, "You are only upset about a castor oil plant which cost you no labor, which you did not make grow, which sprouted in a night and has perished in a night. And am I not to feel sorry for Nineveh, the great city, in which there are more than a hundred and twenty thousand people who cannot tell their right hand from their left, to say nothing of all the animals?"

Yes, the Jonah-like vexation still is with us. There are always people who commit themselves selflessly and tirelessly, and over whom the wheel of history seems to run mindlessly. After a period of great attention, they are simply forgotten. What they as poet, novelist, or scientist had to proclaim is judged no longer interesting. They are laid aside. They no longer play a role. How understandable it is when these people pull sulkily back into a corner to build, as Jonah did, a shelter for themselves. They take off for the "east," outside the city—that is, away from the traffic of the world. They feel themselves unjustly treated by fate. And from the point of view of the self, their complaint is often justified. It is, however, not justified if one contemplates the situation from the greater distance of effective prophetic proclamation. According to our mode of interpretation, the story is telling us that Jonah falls into a crisis of the soul after his star has faded from the public eye. And again in his aloneness and retreat he discovers new and forceful insight.

Here the symbol of the castor oil plant becomes central. This plant which God made grow on one day and allowed to be destroyed the next represents the human person. Both, the text seems to say, can grow to an extraordinary and wondrous size. But the worm of disappointment and the dry east wind of quarrelsomeness can completely destroy this magnificence. Even though narcissistic self is understandable, it functions positively only when it points to the need in the individual. Then there is again the possibility of addressing the rest of creation, even the great city of Nineveh itself.

This last section of the Jonah story demonstrates the prophetic pattern of unbelief, relapse into self-pity, and finally the renewal of priority for the survival of all humankind. It is this final stage which allows room for the confirmation of the person within the historical process.

4.

Concerning the Myth About the Marriages of the Angels

Right before the Biblical account of the flood, there is a short story which even today exegetes characterize as "an obscure passage" (note in the Jerusalem Bible). The flood, of course, is presented as God's punishment of humankind which had become evil. But immediately before that story is the one we consider here:

> When men had become plentiful on the earth, and daughters had been born to them, the sons of God, looking at the daughters of men, saw they were pleasing, so they married as many as they chose. Yahweh said, "My spirit must not forever be disgraced in man, for he is but flesh; his life shall last no more than a hundred and twenty years." The Nephilim were on the earth at that time (and even afterward) when the sons of God resorted to the daughters of man, and had children by them. These are the heroes of days gone by, the famous men.

What in the world are "sons of God"? And how can we understand these events and that humankind is punished for something that someone supposedly from God has done? For the text is clear on that point. It is punishment in two senses. First, the length of human life is reduced. Then, practically the whole race is destroyed by the flood. What kind of unforgivable crime are we dealing with here? And what does it all have to do with these strange beings at the end of the passage? Luther's translation calls them tyrants. Other translators simply transliterate the Hebrew *nephilim.* Still others use "the huge ones" or "the titans."

In the history of exegesis the "sons of God" have gone through many interpretations. This confused history has to a certain extent hidden the primary fact, that they are of mythical origin. This eliminates right away the so-called "Sethite interpretation," which maintains that they are the progeny of Seth, Cain's younger brother. Then there is the "potentate interpretation" of Jewish heritage: "The sons of God are the affluent and powerful people, while the daughters of men are women of lower class" (Oswald Loretz, *Schöpfung und Mythos,* pp. 32 ff.; Stuttgart, 1968). No matter how one has sought to explain the passage in terms of primitive social order or Biblicistic historiography, the result has always been less than satisfactory. But it has certainly been uncomfortable for the church fathers to deal with the suggestion that the gods sought sexual relations with the daughters of men. Of course, there is no real way around the sexuality in the passage, since the daughters of men bore the sons of God's children. And these children, the passage says in hushed tones, belonged to a race of giants, or at least of extraordinary power. All these difficulties have obviously led to a shortening of the text, which itself confuses the issue even more. How it may have originally sounded and that it really is an old mythical declaration becomes clear when one compares the following passage from The Book of Enoch.

And it happened that as the children of men began to become more numerous on the surface of the earth, and they bore daughters, the angels of God saw them in a year of Jubilee. They saw that the daughters of men were beautiful to look at, and they took the ones they wanted as wives. And they bore children of the angels, and these are the giants. And violence increased on the earth, and all flesh became corrupt, from the people to the cattle and the

65

animals and the birds, indeed everything that walked on the earth. They became spoiled and immoral and began to devour one another. And violence increased on the earth, and all the thoughts of people were evil at all times. And God spoke: I want to exterminate humanity and all flesh on the face of the earth which I have made. And Noah alone found favor in the sight of God. And God was very angry with the angels which he had sent to earth. And he commanded that they be eradicated and removed from their duties. And he told us to bind them in the depths of the earth. And behold, they are bound there and are kept there. And the word from his countenance went forth over their children that he wanted to pierce them with a sword and expel them from heaven. And he spoke: "My spirit will not always rest with humankind. For they are flesh, and their days shall be a hundred and twenty years."

Our difficulties are largely avoided when we steer clear of the dead end of seeking the correct literal interpretation. For The Book of Enoch makes it clearer that we are dealing here with an ancient myth. Here also the story is more understandable. Gods and human women unite sexually to produce giants or half-gods with special gifts and power.

This myth is as old as humankind itself. Heracles, the son of the god Zeus and the human woman Alcmene, is the best-known example of this myth. The idea of demigods comes possibly from a people's experience of unusually spiritually and physically powerful individuals, especially leaders. Correctly these individuals appeared to their contemporaries to have an unearthly charisma. They seemed to be the incarnation of gods in people. That was especially the case when the heroes of the group enabled the society to attain a new level of consciousness or cultural development. It seemed improbable and in reality absurd that such an extraordinary power could come from an ordinary father. This is most probably the way the myth of the virgin birth developed. In terms of the history of personal development, the birth of the heroes corresponds to the strengthening of the ego in persons. This strengthening marks both progress and danger for the person. Erich Neumann has emphasized this relationship, and Uwe Steffen has reinforced the point. He writes:

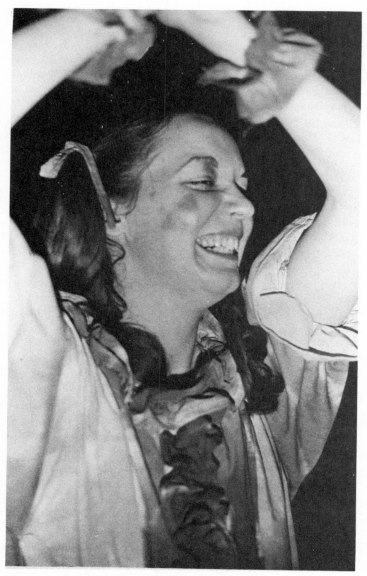

In terms of the history of personal development, the birth of the heroes corresponds to the strengthening of the ego in persons

The birth of the hero is always a virgin birth, since the extraordinary and totally other nature of the hero marks in myth the birth of the "higher man," which belongs with consciousness, ego, and will. His symbol is the head and the eye. The higher manhood comes mythologically to expression in the characterization of the hero as the son of a god, the power of heaven. Since the power of heaven is mythologically male, the hero becomes the son of God. As representative of the generative spiritual world, he is the herald of the new. The hero is therefore the ego-hero. His battle against the dragon is a battle of the ego consciousness against the power of the unconscious.

But the deeds of these heroes lead to blessing only when they do not misuse their special gifts and place themselves on the level of God. Basically the myth of the angels' marriages is connected with the myth of creation. For the creation myth states that God breathed life into Adam and therefore made humanity unique in creation as his co-creator. But this "equality" signifies the gift of freedom to human beings, a gift that carries with it the danger of arbitrariness and arrogant separation from God.

Especially when compared to the virgin birth the story of the angels' marriages makes it clear that the "hero" comes from the combining of the divine spirit and the earthly substance. This combination alone can make humanity blessed, and then only when it is placed in the service of God. If one uses the power of these special gifts or intelligence to attribute self-congratulatory divine powers to one's self, then the heart of humanity's potential is corrupted. This same characteristic of arbitrariness appears in the story of the angels' marriages when the angels decide for themselves to take the daughters of men as their wives. Here apparently is the commencement of the rebellion. This stands in marked contrast to the story of the virgin birth, where it expressly stated that the pregnancy is sent from God. In that story the angel is a serving angel, not a self-serving being. Just as in the disobedience of Adam and Eve and in the theft of fire by Prometheus, the actions of the sons of God are punished. In each case the eye is on self-serving enjoyment, not God and his creation. The punishment consists consequently of a limiting of the possible power of human beings, because they have demonstrated that they only misuse their freedom. This is symbolically expressed in the limiting of the life-span of people. The basic message is this: Selfish use of spiritual potential without remaining in relationship to God produces a presumptuousness which does not raise consciousness. Rather, it seems to lead to a narrowing of perspective which during certain periods of history eventually destroys the self.

This message pertains to our lives too. We also live with self-willed presumptuousness, proud desire, and an idolized lust.

The expression "giants" or "titans" is further indication that our interpretation is on the right track. For the Titans of Greece were also powerful beings who had fallen and become phantoms of destruction. The myth of the "giants" also contains the symbol for supernatural power which has become violent and destructive. Luther's translation of *nephilim* as "tyrants" really contains this same message. There are individuals who use their great power arbitrarily, selfishly, and destructively. By doing so, they call God's creation into question. Only in Enoch's story, however, is it directly stated that these Nephilim and heroes of a primeval time are the giant products of the mating of the sons of God and the daughters of men. That of course makes sense in mythological terms.

But God's anger must consequently be directed against such people and their deified heroes, for what occurs is a *misuse* of the very spirit which enables humanity to develop (to produce "spirit children"). This misuse endangers creation and leads, our text says, directly to the corruption of the faithless.

Again this truth holds for us. We all knew it so personally as we crawled out of the Noah's ark of the Second World War, after Hitler's gruesome annihilation. We knew again about the punishment of the flood, and the disaster which breaks over humankind when it follows ego-inflated leaders.

That the issue is megalomania, the power-grabbing by human beings, is confirmed by the story that parallels the one about the angels' marriages. The story of the tower of Babel speaks clearly also of the dangers of being free humans. Here is the text itself:

> Throughout the earth men spoke the same language, with the same vocabulary. Now as they moved eastward they found a plain in the land of Shinar where they settled. They said to one another, "Come, let us make bricks and bake them in fire." For stone they used bricks, and for mortar they used bitumen. "Come," they said, "let us build ourselves a town and a tower with its top reaching heaven. Let us make a name for ourselves, so that we may not be scattered about the whole earth."
>
> Now Yahweh came down to see the town and the tower that the sons of man had built. "So they are all a single people with a single language," said Yahweh. "This is but the start of their undertakings. There will be nothing too hard for them to do. Come, let us go down and confuse their language on the spot so that they can no longer understand one another." Yahweh scattered them thence over the face of the earth, and they stopped building the town. It was named Babel therefore, because there Yahweh confused the language of the whole earth. It was from there that Yahweh scattered them over the whole face of the earth.

In the tower of Babel we see the symbol of humanity's own attempt at independent creation. In terms of depth psychology the tower is a phallus symbol. Because of its shape, it represents the impregnating and creative power of the male which the penis is. The tower can be—as it is in the many wondrous church towers and domes—a symbol of the creative power of God or the creative link between God and humans, between heaven and earth. It can also, however, be a spiteful demonstration of human arrogance. In any case this is what the story of Babel is referring to. The tower becomes such a danger to people that God deems it necessary to confuse the builders. That is, the megalomania of humanity is met with the ineffectiveness of the human intellect. Through this lessening of human intelligence God intends to limit the danger that human beings will destroy creation through the misuse of their freedom.

What a wonderful picture this is for our time, when one

thinks of the gray, logical, dismembering learnedness of our scientists. It is indeed comforting to recognize that their own inability to make their theories understandable is a precaution of the Creator against their own potential for power-grabbing.

The opposite to such arrogance and self-aggrandizement is the model of Christ. Although the heart of the virgin birth myth holds true (as product of Father God and the Virgin Mary he represents the incarnation of the divine in humanity), Christ's life serves only creation. Through faithfulness and obedience he effects the reality of spirit in matter.

5.

Jacob and Joseph:
The Story of
Psychic Transformation

In the interpretation of depth psychology, the figure of Jacob in the Old Testament provides us with a remarkable unity. The stages of his life correspond almost exactly to the patterns of our soul's development. This becomes apparent when we put our theory to work that the figures around Jacob are unconscious elements in his own soul. Using this approach, we discover in the story of Jacob a definite process of individuation portrayed in mythical images.

With the help of his mother, Rebecca, the story says, Jacob swindles the birthright from his older brother and their blind father. Many other Biblical stories tell of "the firstborn." Often there is a command to sacrifice the firstborn. In Job the monster Behemoth is characterized as the "firstborn" of God's way. The firstborn Esau is, as in the parable of the prodigal son, a good man. He is especially known for his hairiness. To disguise Jacob as Esau, Rebecca covers him with animal skins so that the blind father will not notice the trickery. We see here that the trickery of Jacob is a variation on the first great motif of the Bible—disobedient humanity breaking out of paradise. In place of the apple-eating Adam, there is Jacob. In place of Eve and the snake, there is Rebecca. And in place of God, there is the blind father. Esau replaces the earth out of which Adam is made. Basically one could also say that the figures of Cain and Abel are repeated, here with more differentiation in the persons of Esau and Jacob. Esau embodies that aspect of us which has adapted completely to the basic order of God. He is still very "bestial" (he has much hair), because he, like the animals, follows unconsciously the biologically determined laws of creation. Erich Neumann names this "firstborn status" of the soul's development "the stage of the inclusion of the ego in the unconscious." The second son, Jacob, marks the soul's development into a new stage. This is the stage of the freeing and assertion of the ego and the conscious out of unconsciousness. This ego is for that reason "finer" than Esau. It has an almost hairless human skin. Here also, as in the image of the eaten fruit from Eden, the primeval order is disturbed by theft and cunning. There begins to be a lack of unity of human development, noticeable even during pregnancy as the child begins to kick and move. Rebecca's pregnancy is described in the following manner:

> But the children struggled with one another inside her, and she said, "If this is the way of it, why go on living?" So she went to consult Yahweh, and he said to her: "There are two nations in your womb, your issue will be two rival peoples. One nation shall have the mastery of the other, and the elder shall serve the younger."

In the development of each person there are such signs of unrest, sleeplessness, and hectic impulse to move which are forebodings of a coming change.

As in the story of the Fall, we discover here a secret, yet desired, necessity within. Rebecca, the great Mother Nature herself, initiates this process, just as rebellion today is characteristic of the bodily maturation process which occurs during puberty. "From the *it* should develop the *I,*" Freud said in describing this unavoidable development of the soul. Jacob's theft of the birthright means that the ego now reinforced with consciousness takes over the direction of the whole person. Next, both in the story and in human development the irresistible happens. And it happens at the cost of the unity of the person. The instinctive part, which until now has dominated and functioned in a natural, yet unconscious, way, is devalued, dethroned, and, in the language of modern psychology, repressed. Exactly because the birth of the ego out of matter is an instinctive event, the ego's strengthening must result in nature's repression. The young and weak ego could not coexist with the insight into the immoral. It would be destroyed unless it is strengthened. A person in this stage is proud of his accomplishment, holds himself in too high esteem, and thinks of himself as diligent and good. That person does not see his shadowed side.

This psychic status is dangerous. When Esau suspects that he has been cheated, he contemplates strangling Jacob. This image portrays the inner conflict which defends itself against all possibilities of injury to the weak ego. One's guard is put up against a flood of unconscious feedback, since that might produce a slipping back into the primeval lack of consciousness. All this is expressed in Esau's intention to murder Jacob. This condition results in a further split between the ego and the unconscious. Its occurrence is simply a matter of survival of the self. For that reason it is the mother, Rebecca (the primeval mother of instincts), who recommends that her son flee in order to avoid being strangled. A strengthened ego that has distinguished itself from its drives and instincts has a good chance in the world. It can enact plans and thoughts in order to accomplish egotistic goals, thereby undergirding the ego even more. Jacob's maneuvering and becoming rich in the territory of his father-in-law, Laban, illustrates that. The many women, the big herds, and the twelve children express the enormous growth through experience, knowledge, and intelligence which occurs at this stage.

But every expansion of the ego has its limits. A person cannot flee his shadow during an entire life-span of undifferentiating assertions. If the development of the soul is not to stagnate, the person needs to reflect on the motives of his behavior. The person needs a self-awareness that addresses his own power problem. One needs to explain one's own functioning. In our story this happens exactly on schedule in an encounter between Jacob and Esau. And the ego of this new Adam survives the test of its development by anticipating the event with fear, attention, and humility. The situation is pictured in the following manner:

Jacob sent messengers ahead of him to his brother Esau in the land of Seir, the countryside of Edom, with these instructions, "Say this to my lord Esau, 'Here is the message of your servant Jacob: I have been staying with Laban till now, and have acquired oxen, beasts of burden and flocks, and men and women slaves. I send news of this to my lord in the hope of winning your approval.'" The messengers returned to Jacob and told him, "We went to your brother Esau, and he is already on his way to meet you; there are four hundred men with him."

Jacob was greatly afraid and distressed. He divided the people with him, and the flocks and cattle, into two companies, saying, "If Esau comes to one of the companies and attacks it, the other company will be left to escape." Jacob said, "O God of my father Abraham, and God of my father Isaac, Yahweh who said to me, 'Go back to your country and family, and I will make you prosper,' I am unworthy of all the kindness and goodness you have shown your servant. I had only my staff when I crossed the Jordan here, and now I can form two companies. I implore you, save me from my brother's clutches, for I am afraid of him; he may come and attack us and the mothers and their children. Yet it was you who said, 'I will make you prosper, and make your descendants like the sand on the seashore, so many that it cannot be counted.'" Then Jacob passed the night there.

From what he had with him he chose a gift for his brother Esau: two hundred she-goats and twenty he-goats, two hundred ewes and twenty rams, thirty camels in milk with their calves, forty cows and ten bulls, twenty she-asses and ten donkeys. He put them in the charge of his servants, in separate droves, and he told his servants, "Go ahead of me, leaving a space between each drove and the next." He gave the first this order: "When my brother Esau meets you and asks, 'To whom do you belong? Where are you going? Whose are those animals that you are driving?' you will answer, 'To your servant Jacob. They are a gift sent to my lord Esau. Jacob himself is following.' " He gave the same order to the second and the third, and to all who were following the droves, "That is what you must say to Esau when you find him. You must say, 'Yes, your servant Jacob himself is following.' " For he argued, "I shall conciliate him by sending a gift in advance; so when I come face to face with him he may perhaps receive me favorably." The gift went ahead of him, but he himself spent that night in the camp.

Jacob's readiness to give so much of his riches to Esau is typical characterization of the beginning of what C. G. Jung calls the process of individuation. At that stage the person must reduce his will to power in order to effect reconciliation with his unconscious. The sacrifice, a conscious reduction of external power, is the requirement for inner wholeness and maturation of the person. This potential encounters all of us in the second half of our lives. The sacrifice involves a hard fight with one's self. It sends one to the brink of breakdown. It means a readiness to conquer one's own self-praise and power-grabbing. This is the borderline situation which is so wonderfully pictured in the fight between Jacob and the angel. The text goes this way:

> That same night he rose, and taking his two wives and his two slave girls and his eleven children he crossed the ford of the Jabbok. He took them and sent them across the stream and sent all his possessions over too. And Jacob was left alone. And there was one that wrestled with him until daybreak who, seeing that he could not master him, struck him in the socket of his hip, and Jacob's hip was dislocated as he wrestled with him. He said, "Let me go, for day is breaking." But Jacob answered, "I will not let you go unless you bless me." He then asked, "What is your name?" "Jacob," he replied. He said, "Your name shall no longer be Jacob, but Israel, because you have been strong against God, you shall prevail against men." Jacob then made this request, "I beg you, tell me your name," but he replied, "Why do you ask my name?" And he blessed him there. Jacob named the place Peniel, "Because I have seen God face to face," he said, "and I have survived." The sun rose as he left Peniel, limping because of his hip.

At night, which means during a time of the darkness of the soul, a river is crossed. The river is a symbol in depth psychology for boundary situations. And during this night of inner need the process of taking stock happens. Jacob survives it triumphantly. The night battle with the angel at the river and Jacob's vow not to let him go until he has given his blessing indicate that Jacob has successfully conquered his own drive for power. It signifies Jacob's coming to grips with his own limits and his seeking to place himself under God's commands. This "integration of the shadow" makes him a remarkable person, since he has shown himself capable of changing and climbing to another level of awareness. Now it is no longer a matter of furthering one's own profane opportunities. Rather, now the enrichment of one's soul is the primary question. Jacob's limp after the battle expressed the loss of power that one sustains in the external, profane world when one consciously reduces and sacrifices one's own drive for power. The value system of Jacob has been changed. From the "child of the world," as the Bible puts it, comes a "child of light." This rebirth "through water and the spirit" earns Jacob a new name. For that reason the passage reads, "Your name shall no longer be Jacob, but Israel, because you have been strong against God, you shall prevail against men." Our mode of interpretation is confirmed by the fact that immediately after this "crossing over into a new land" Jacob meets his brother Esau and is reconciled to him. Now the "firstborn," the sphere of the instinct, can find again a place in Jacob's soul. But he had first, with his own will and consciousness, to eliminate his own careless will to power.

It is as a result of these processes that now the twelfth son of Jacob, Joseph, who is a new, particularly honorable sprout from Jacob, appears. And Joseph really does simply continue the developmental stages of Jacob. This next stage is characterized by the gift of intuition. This sense for the deep connections in life enriches the personality and enables its completion. This is the hope expressed in Jacob's preference for Joseph. The passage describes it this way:

Israel loved Joseph more than all his other sons, for he was the son of his old age, and he had a coat with long sleeves made for him. But his brothers, seeing how his father loved him more than all his other sons, came to hate him so much that they could not say a civil word to him.

As soon as the capability to intuit appears in a person, he is immediately in great danger. The danger is first of all that his newly acquired gift will make him arrogant, and thereby bring on inner and external conflict. This threat comes as much from the inner world of the soul (where the "other brothers" live) as from the external world. This strengthening of one's intuition does not cause the imbalance of egocentricity. Rather, it can bring on the imbalance of turning completely inward. That can produce circumstances in which the person cuts himself off from the world and loses a sense of reality. The dominance of this introverted side of Joseph is described in the following dream of Joseph:

> Now Joseph had a dream, and he repeated it to his brothers. "Listen," he said, "to this dream I have had. We were binding sheaves in the countryside; and my sheaf, it seemed, rose up and stood upright; then I saw your sheaves gather round and bow to my sheaf." "So you want to be king over us," his brothers retorted, "or to lord it over us?" And they hated him still more, on account of his dreams and of what he said. He had another dream which he told his brothers. "Look, I have had another dream," he said. "I thought I saw the sun, the moon and eleven stars, bowing to me." He told his father and brothers, and his father scolded him. "A fine dream to have!" he said to him. "Are all of us then, myself, your mother and your brothers, to come and bow to the ground before you?" His brothers were jealous of him, but his father kept the thing in mind.

These dreams were the other parts of the soul's warning. They led directly to the elimination of the intuitive side, which, in the picture language of our story, is described as the throwing of

Joseph into a pit and selling him into slavery in Egypt. The story is like this:

> They saw him in the distance, and before he reached them they made a plot among themselves to put him to death. "Here comes the man of dreams," they said to one another. "Come let us kill him and throw him into some well; we can say that a wild beast devoured him. Then we shall see what becomes of his dreams."
>
> But Reuben heard, and he saved him from their violence. "We must not take his life," he said. "Shed no blood," Reuben said to them, "throw him into this well in the wilderness, but do not lay violent hands on him"—intending to save him from them and to restore him to his father. So, when Joseph reached his brother, they pulled off his coat, the coat with long sleeves that he was wearing, and catching hold of him they threw him into the well, an empty well with no water in it. They then sat down to eat.
>
> Looking up they saw a group of Ishmaelites who were coming from Gilead, their camels laden with gum, tragacanth, balsam and resin, which they were taking down into Egypt. Then Judah said to his brothers, "What do we gain by killing our brother and covering up his blood? Come, let us sell him to the Ishmaelites, but let us not do any harm to him. After all, he is our brother, and our own flesh." His brothers agreed.
>
> Now some Midianite merchants were passing, and they drew Joseph up out of the well. They sold Joseph to the Ishmaelites for twenty silver pieces, and these men took Joseph to Egypt. When Reuben went back to the well there was no sign of Joseph. Tearing his clothes, he went back to his brothers. "The boy has disappeared," he said. "What am I going to do?"
>
> They took Joseph's coat and, slaughtering a goat, they dipped the coat in the blood. Then they sent the coat with the long sleeves and had it taken to their father, with the message, "This is what we have found. Examine it and see whether or not it is your son's coat." He examined it and exclaimed, "It is my son's coat! A wild beast has devoured him. Joseph has been the prey of some animal and has been torn to pieces." Jacob, tearing his clothes and putting on a loincloth of sackcloth, mourned his son for a long time. All his sons and daughters came to comfort him, but he refused to be comforted. "No," he said, "I will go down in mourning to Sheol, beside my son." And his father wept for him. Meanwhile the

Midianites had sold him in Egypt to Potiphar, one of Pharaoh's officials and commander of the guard.

The process of repressing the intuitive side of the soul leads to a definite inner brokenness, because the intuitive is absolutely needed for the further development of the soul. Individual parts of the soul disintegrate into habitual lying and self-deception. (The brothers deceived their father concerning Joseph's actual fate.) Some people become depressed in such a state (the father), others become brutal (Judah) when the conscience (Reuben) comes on too strong. And the most noble part (as a result of repression) is banished to the unconscious (the imprisonment of Joseph). Such a disappointment with oneself leads quite readily to external isolation. This isolation for the intuitive person is like "seven fat years" despite its lack of consciousness. There follows a storing up of energy for the soul. This energy becomes all the stronger when Joseph withstands an attempt to allay the energy with the sexual drive (the temptation of Potiphar's wife).

In this situation now where the intuitive function is still powerfully repressed (Joseph's servitude) two significant dreams become signposts for the way to development. First we learn in the story, however, that a baker and a cupbearer who have fallen out of grace with the king wind up in the same jail as Joseph.

In the individuation process the rise of a new king (here the Pharaoh) is a sign that the old ego has been conquered and that the soul is ruled by a new order. Jung named this the "self." Here all the opposites in the psyche are unified under a superpersonal principle. But this integration of all functions into a wholeness is a troublesome matter. Each individual drive requires in this process a special formation and nourishment. How that relates to the drive for nourishment is portrayed in the following dreams of the baker and the cupbearer.

It happened some time later that the king of Egypt's cupbearer and his baker offended their master the king of Egypt. Pharaoh was angry with his two officials, the chief cupbearer and the chief baker, and put them under arrest in the house of the commander of the guard, in the jail where Joseph was a prisoner. The commander of the guard assigned Joseph to them to attend to their wants, and they remained under arrest for some time.

Now both of them had dreams on the same night, each with its own meaning for the cupbearer and the baker of the king of Egypt, who were prisoners in the jail. When Joseph came to them in the morning, he saw that they looked gloomy, and he asked the two officials who were with him under arrest in the master's house, "Why these dark looks today?" They answered him, "We have had a dream, but there is no one to interpret it." "Are not interpretations God's business?" Joseph asked them. "Come, tell me."

So the chief cupbearer described his dream to Joseph, telling him, "In my dream I saw a vine in front of me. On the vine were three branches; no sooner had it budded than it blossomed, and its clusters became ripe grapes. I had Pharaoh's cup in my hand; I picked the grapes and squeezed them into Pharaoh's cup, and put the cup into Pharaoh's hand." "Here is the interpretation of it," Joseph told him. "The three branches are three days. In another three days Pharaoh will release you and restore you to your place. Then you will hand Pharaoh his cup, as you did before, when you were his cupbearer. But be sure to remember me when things go well with you, and do me the kindness of reminding Pharaoh about me, to get me out of this house. I was kidnapped from the land of the Hebrews in the first place, and even here I have done nothing to warrant imprisonment."

The chief baker, seeing that the interpretation had been favorable, said to Joseph, "I too had a dream; there were three trays of cakes on my head. In the top tray there were all kinds of Pharaoh's favorite cakes, but the birds ate them off the tray on my head." Joseph gave him this answer, "Here is the interpretation of it: the three trays are three days. In another three days Pharaoh will release you and hang you on a gallows, and the birds will eat the flesh off your bones."

And so it happened; the third day was Pharaoh's birthday and he gave a great banquet for all his officials, and he released the chief cupbearer, to hand Pharaoh his cup; the chief baker he hanged. It was as Joseph had said in his interpretation. But the chief cupbearer did not remember Joseph: he forgot him.

The image of the baker and the cupbearer sinning signifies the prevailing of the drive for nourishment. Eating and drinking too much are often compensatory satisfaction in crisis situations. They are in these cases exaggerated and can lead to a misuse of the "oral" function. Here the development of the personalities is so far along that the misuse of appetite and thirst is responded to. The baker and the cupbearer are thrown into prison, symbolizing the repression of the drives. The dreams and their interpretation by the intuitive side of the person (Joseph) show that it is necessary to kill the primitive side of the drive for nourishment (the baker) while bringing the spiritual side (the cupbearer) to expression. C. G. Jung directs us to such an interpretation of bread and wine. He writes: "Concerning the special natural substances, bread is doubtless a means of nourishment. Wine 'strengthens' one also, but in a different sense than as a means of nourishment. It stimulates and 'causes the heart of a person to rejoice.' Wine has then a certain volatile quality which we call 'spirit.' It is dissimilar to harmless water, because a 'spirit' or 'god' lives in it, which brings on an addictive ecstasy. The miracle of Cana was at the same time the miracle at the temple of Dionysus. And it lends a deeper meaning to see Christ depicted on the Damascus eucharistic chalice, enthroned among vine tendrils, like Dionysus. As bread represents the physical means of existence, so wine portrays the spiritual life." (Carl Gustav Jung, *Von den Wurzeln des Unbewussten,* Ch. 5; Zurich, 1954.)

The primacy of the religious spirit in the person effects a raising of consciousness and with that (after a period of latent development represented by the cupbearer's forgetfulness) a recognition of the value of the intuitive. The intuitive is seen then as essential in personal development, because it has an especially fine connection with the instinctive regions of the soul. Intuition is the soul's organ for seeing. It contains traces of the other parts of the soul, and therefore is important in the soul's relationship to the future. For this reason it can determine the meaning of Pharaoh's dreams about the seven full and the seven dry ears of grain, and the seven fat cows swallowed by the seven thin ones. Strengthened by the stillness of isolation and the working together with social efficacy (Pharaoh), the soul enters a new creative phase (the fruitful seven years). Here the soul gains strength from all its successive phases, and summons its various now developed aspects to overcome a final disaster (the seven lean years). The division of the person, the raising up of the ego (Jacob), the coarse regions of endurance (the brothers), the impoverishment of inner life—all are drawn upon as the intuitive powers are collected (the granaries) to meet successfully the final crisis. This is followed by the picture of the journey of the brothers to Egypt, which represents the insight and recognition of the necessity and superiority of the intuitive. The unity of the soul is restored (the father moves to Egypt with all his children) through repentance. The soul now recognizes its true guide in the intuitive spirit (Joseph's leadership in Egypt).

6.

The Tree of Life

Yes, the Holy Scriptures are full of dreamlike imagery. That, we have seen clearly enough in the preceding chapters. But the Bible's profound connection with the world of dreams does not end here. Not only is there this imagery. There are also many actual dreams in the Scriptures. Often the importance of this kind of communication is stressed by wise and prophetic witnesses.

The Old Testament abounds in stories of seers who are called before kings to interpret dreams. The seers discover in the dreams the course of the country's future. This then allows the king to react strategically to the coming events.

Contemporary dream researchers, above all C. G. Jung and his school, have come up with strikingly similar data. They also encounter prophetic dreams which act as warnings of major societal events such as wars and natural catastrophes. But these contemporary prophetic dreams seem limited generally to subjective developments. With regularity, dreams foresee change and growth within a person.

The Book of Daniel reports the dream of King Nebuchadnezzar. The prophet Belteshazzar recognizes readily the dream of the king as having to do with the king's own person.

The prophet understands that the dream makes a new level of personal consciousness available. And this new consciousness anticipates the future.

Interestingly enough, this dream focuses on a symbol which modern dream interpretation lays great emphasis on. This image in the ancient king's dream, the tree, happens also to be centrally important in what today's researchers call projective diagnosis of dreams. So this dream seems especially promising as a way of showing us new possibilities of understanding the symbolic mode of expression.

The text describes the dream and related events:

"I saw a tree in the middle of the world; it was very tall. The tree grew taller and stronger, until its top reached the sky, and it could be seen from the ends of the earth. Its foliage was beautiful, its fruit abundant, in it was food for all. For the wild animals it provided shade, the birds of heaven nested in its branches, all living creatures found their food on it. I watched the visions passing through my head as I lay in bed. Next a watcher, a holy one came down from heaven. At the top of his voice he shouted, 'Cut the tree down, lop off its branches, strip off its leaves, throw away its fruit; let the animals flee from its shelter and the birds from its branches. But leave stump and roots in the ground bound with hoops of iron and bronze in the grass of the field. Let him be drenched with the dew of heaven, let him share the grass of the earth with the animals. Let his heart turn from mankind, let a beast's heart be given him and seven times pass over him. Such is the sentence proclaimed by the watchers, the verdict announced by the holy ones, that every living creature may learn that the Most High rules over the kingship of men, he confers it on whom he pleases and raises the lowest of mankind.'

"This is the dream I had, I, Nebuchadnezzar the king. Now it is for you, Belteshazzar, to pronounce on its meaning, since not one of the sages in my kingdom has been able to interpret it for me; you, however, will be able to, because the spirit of God Most Holy resides in you."

Daniel, known as Belteshazzar, hesitated for a moment in embarrassment. The king said, "Belteshazzar, do not be alarmed at the dream and its meaning." Belteshazzar answered, "My lord, may the dream apply to your enemies, and its meaning to your foes. The tree you saw that grew so tall and strong that it reached the sky and could be seen from the ends of the earth, the tree with beautiful foliage and abundant fruit, with food for all in it, providing shade for the wild animals, with the birds of heaven nesting in its branches, that tree is yourself,O king, for you have grown tall and strong; your stature is now so great that it reaches the sky, and your rule extends to the ends of the earth.

"And the watcher seen by the king, the holy one coming down from heaven and saying, 'Cut the tree down and destroy it, but leave stump and roots in the ground, bound with hoops of iron and bronze in the grass of the field; let him be drenched with the dew of heaven, let him share with the wild animals until seven times have passed over him': the meaning of this, O king, this decree of the Most High passed on my lord the king, is this:

"You are to be driven from human society and live with the wild animals; you will feed on grass like oxen, you will be drenched by the dew of heaven; seven times will pass over you until you have learned that the Most High rules over the kingship of men, and confers it on whom he pleases.

"And the order, 'Leave the stump and roots of the tree,' means that your kingdom will be kept for you until you come to understand that heaven rules all. May it please the king to accept my advice: by virtuous actions break with your sins, break with your crimes by showing mercy to the poor, and so live long and peacefully."

This all happened to King Nebuchadnezzar. Twelve months later, while strolling on the roof of the royal palace in Babylon, the king was saying, "Great Babylon! Imperial palace! Was it not built by me alone, by my own might and power to the glory of my majesty?" The boast was not out of his mouth when a voice came down from heaven: "King Nebuchadnezzar, these words are for you! Sovereignty is taken from you, you are to be driven from human society, and live with the wild animals; you will feed on grass like oxen, and seven times will pass over you until you have learned that the Most High rules over the kingship of men, and confers it on whom he pleases."

The words were immediately fulfilled: Nebuchadnezzar was driven from human society and fed on grass like oxen, and was drenched by the dew of heaven; his hair grew as long as eagle's feathers, and his nails became like bird's claws.

"When the time was over, I, Nebuchadnezzar, lifted up my

eyes to heaven: my reason returned. And I blessed the Most High, praising and extolling him who lives forever, for his sovereignty is an eternal sovereignty, his empire lasts from age to age. The inhabitants of the earth count for nothing: he does as he pleases with the array of heaven, and with the inhabitants of the earth. No one can arrest his hand or ask him, 'What are you doing?'

"At that moment my reason returned, and, to the glory of my royal state, my majesty and splendor returned too. My counselors and noblemen acclaimed me; I was restored to my throne, and to my greatness even more was added. And now I, Nebuchadnezzar, praise and extol and glorify the King of heaven, his promises are always faithfully fulfilled, his ways are always just, and he has power to humble those who walk in pride."

It doesn't matter in this instance whether we consider the king and the interpreter of his dream as one person. In any case the arbitrary pride of power, the old ego, is in control of King Nebuchadnezzar. He has shown real development as king, but now, because of his own extravagance, he is in danger of being cut down. However, the humiliation of the king happens only after he continues his haughty stance rather than follow the warning of the dream interpreter (or shall we say, of his own intuition?). His lust for power ends up unleashing his unconscious; that is, his grasping for power becomes so unrealistic and so uncontrollable (he received the heart of an animal) that he is classified as "insane" and removed from his position.

The tree still is a symbol for the state of people's lives. In fact, in my practice I encountered a dream that parallels Nebuchadnezzar's. A twenty-year-old man who sought counseling because of failure in school had the following dream after his first session:

"I am standing in front of a tree. But it is cut down. The ax is still stuck in the tree's stump. There are drops of blood on it." When asked what strikes him about this picture, the young man says, "I too feel as though I have been cut down, since I have had to repeat the same class twice and now am told I must leave school."

This dream told me that this young person was in great danger of sinking into depression and of trying to take his own life. The dream horrified me, much as Nebuchadnezzar's dream had horrified Daniel. But through this tremendous warning all our awareness was mobilized. After a few months the young man had overcome his defeatist stance and found strength for new initiatives in his life.

Trees are not only symbols of negative developments in the lives of our contemporaries. Often girls dream that they are standing in front of a tree full of ripe cherries just before they have their first menstrual period. Before her wedding a young woman saw an apple tree. She knew that the tree was ready for harvest.

A forty-year-old woman told me of a dream in which she saw the branches of a leafy tree suddenly begin to grow inward. All around the tree there were diapers flapping in the wind. I asked her if she was pregnant. Shocked, she gave me a definite "No!" Fourteen days later she told me that her menstruation had not come and that she had just been diagnosed as pregnant. Her tree of life and its roots in the unconscious had recognized the coming again of motherhood before such knowledge was possible on a conscious level. Her tree of life had known already that she was approaching once again a time of inner growth.

Christ uses the picture of a tree in a number of parables. There is the fig tree, whose value is evident by its fruits. If it produces unusable fruit, it is cut down. In other words, people who refuse to work with the givens of creation will be considered worthless before God.

The fact that the tree is an archetypal symbol for the development and state of the person has been used in clinical psychology. In the so-called tree test a person draws a fruit tree on a piece of DIN-A, 8" × 11" paper. From the drawing a number of observations about the drawer's life can be made. None of the observations depend in any way on the artistic talents of the drawer.

The trees drawn by neglected young people are intricate, but sloppy and confused—projections of the tired and unordered indifference of the youths themselves. Wirelike trees, such as espalier fruit trees, are drawn by domineered children.

Cracks, sawed-off limbs, and knotholes in a tree reveal wounds to the soul of the drawer. A robust psyche can also be detected from the drawings of the tree. My own work with patients who draw trees parallels and complements the results of Karl Koch, the originator of the tree test.

But the drawing of a tree does not only inform us of the inner life of the drawer. The "tree of life" is related to the primary symbol for the Christian life. Karl Koch has also seen this. He writes:

"The image of the tree possesses a strong evocative character. It calls up within the drawer subjective pictures which melt into the focal object. The drawing contains something of the objective world which at the same time has an integral relationship to the world of the soul. The basic schema of the tree is the cross. This is no projection from the outside. Above and below, to the left and to the right, the four-membered cross corresponds to the tree as much as it matches the figure of a person with outstretched arms. The same symbol is behind both of them. As such, that same symbol becomes something which transcends the individual case. It is the accessibility to realness, concrete and picturable, yet at the same time spiritual, which distinguishes the symbol from conceptual language. Symbols come into being through the likeness of the seeable to the spiritual world. The early Christian theology of symbols had such a comparison at its roots. The early Christians asserted that all of God's revelation in the Old Testament (from the tree of life in Gen. 2:9 to the personalized Wisdom of God in whom the tree of life is embodied in Prov. 3:18) is spoken only while gazing toward the coming saving event. That event which summarizes and fulfills the Old Testament is the death of the incarnated Wisdom on the New Testament tree, the cross. Between the tree of life in paradise and the tree of life in the new heaven the early Christian sees one other tree rising up. This tree, on which the fate of Adam's family hangs, is the cross. This cross is the focal point of the world and of the drama of humankind's salvation." (Karl Koch, *Der Baumtest;* Bern and Stuttgart, 1954.)

From very different points of departure modern clinical psy-

Between the tree of life in paradise and the tree of life in the new heaven the early Christian sees one other tree rising up. This tree, on which the fate of Adam's family hangs, is the cross

chology and Biblical symbolism converge on the same fundamental insight:

In the discovery of the eternal nature of life, humankind encounters its own significance. This discovery occurs through the development of our vital drives. It is paradoxically through sacrifice that these vital drives develop. The symbol for this transformation, this growth through giving away, this life through death, is that unique tree, the cross.

7.

The Parables of Christ as Orientation in the Solution of Central Problems in Life Today

Christ also knew that the picture language of the soul is more basic than the rational-logical mode of thought and possesses an immediate route of access to our feelings and our unconscious. He used this knowledge consciously in the telling of parables in order to reach people's conscience at the feeling level. He knew that this language of images provided a real point of entry into people's lives. To the question of his disciples concerning why he spoke in parables, Jesus said this exactly: "They see and see again, but do not perceive; they hear and hear again, but do not understand." Many parables are interpreted by Jesus himself immediately after he tells them. In these cases there appears to be no difficulty in understanding their particular symbolic meaning. Therefore we will look only for certain uninterpreted parables, especially those which have something to say about the meaning of our life. For it is the search for meaning which is especially poignant for many today. Perhaps additional notes from depth psychology can provide an even more helpful angle on orienting oneself in today's world.

In ch. 13 of Matthew, Jesus presents a number of parables: Here they are:

> The kingdom of heaven is like treasure hidden in a field which someone has found; he hides it again, goes off happy, sells everything he owns and buys the field.
>
> Again, the kingdom of heaven is like a merchant looking for fine pearls; when he finds one of great value he goes and sells everything he owns and buys it.

The text is concerned about the "kingdom of heaven." In the language of the soul the kingdom of heaven is in no way a kingdom of space which is separated from the planet earth. It is, rather, the "above" as contrasted with the "below," aspiring as contrasted with broadening, the heights as compared with the plains, the worthwhile as contrasted with the ordinary, and the perfect as contrasted with the incomplete.

This "higher realm" is now described in pictures by our text. First, the kingdom of heaven is like a hidden treasure. In myths and fairy tales, a treasure represents something of high value, which makes one rich and meets all one's needs. This thing of value is to be found, our passage says, in a field. There is no doubt that the field represents our life's work in the world. In the words of Christ that "the field is the world" (Matt. 13:38), our interpretation is his also. The kingdom of heaven is therefore not to be found in some kind of unreal distant place. Rather, the most valuable thing is to be found in our life. Interestingly enough, the parable says very little about the nature of this valuable object. In the companion parable the pearl details a little more, indicating that the treasured value has to do with beauty and perfection. But instead of detailing this, the parable describes a series of human exchanges. These exchanges are characterized as seeking, finding, hiding, selling, and buying. The kingdom of heaven is not pictured as some kind of static endpoint on the other side of this earthly life. It is, rather, a dynamic and earthly process. The need to seek this value and to guard it is emphasized. But the major accent is on the radical and absolute difference and separation between the old and the new. The farmer and the merchant of the parable gamble everything on this one possibility. They sell all their goods and buy the field or the pearl. The kingdom of heaven, the Scripture

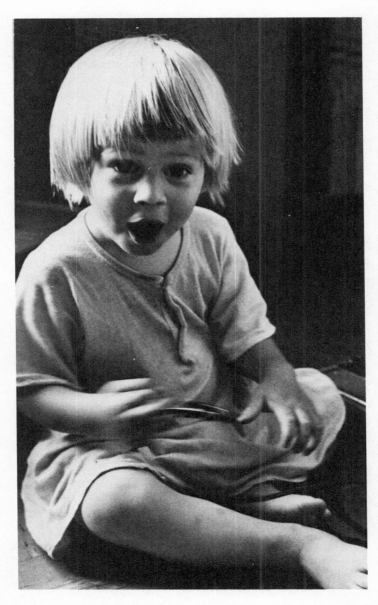

"The kingdom of heaven is like treasure hidden in a field . . ."

says, consists of integrating all values into and under the primacy of the most worthwhile.

One cannot simply dispense with such a teaching. Today we are of the opinion that seeking the "kingdom of heaven" is nonsense. By that, modern human beings do not only mean that there is no real eschatological hope. Our day has also given up the search for the highest religious value. Fascinated by the discoveries of sociology and psychology, we stare wide-eyed at the individual causal relationships which pertain to certain human situations. We have discovered so much relativity in this world that we really no longer believe in the existence of the "treasure in the field" or the "perfect pearl," the miracle of completion, symbol of absolute value.

That the search itself is a real part of that final worth appears improbable to us. The joy and fulfillment of the purchase of the pearl is not ours simply because we have begun to seek due to an intellectual misimpression. But to discover this final insight into life's real value is not its full realization, the parable says. A total change in one's own life must ensue. Everything must be lived in the light of the new value.

The significance of such religious and ethical priorities seems to be slipping through our fingers today. We no longer want to decide. No, it is more that we are no longer capable of deciding. We allow ourselves to be drowned in material and tossed about by public opinion. We want to take everything along with us. We want to accept everything without making any decisions. We are glutted with material. Pluralism, tolerance, and objectivity are the slogans which rob us of the ability to make crucial decisions. A chaotic lack of orientation is increasing, while our desires for peace and joy remain unfulfilled. The kingdom of heaven is different. It is an always new call to gather our strength, reject the worthless, and place ourselves under the spirit of love in service to God.

But the longing for the treasure in the depths and for the costly pearl is not completely dead within humankind. Even today there are still the dreamers of the pearl. They often are those who have scattered themselves in the world more than corresponds to their own inner needs. At night in their dreams they seek the wonderful pearl, the symbol of perfect beauty and roundedness of the soul. And the contents of the dreams challenge the dreamer to change the direction of his life. But, our parable says, conscious change is necessary. Individual decisions are the preparations for a final "separation." It is this divorce which the next parable describes.

> Again, the kingdom of heaven is like a dragnet cast into the sea that brings in a haul of all kinds. When it is full, the fishermen haul it ashore; then, sitting down, they collect the good ones in a basket and throw away those that are no use. This is how it will be at the end of time: the angels will appear and separate the wicked from the just to throw them into the blazing furnace where there will be weeping and grinding of teeth.

There is nothing that "doesn't count," the text says. God's justice is perfected in a clear separation of the good from the bad. There is no possibility of avoiding this dragnet of God.

These words of Christ do apply to the fate of the individual on the other side of death. But our mode of interpretation suggests that they also apply to the lives of all people. Persons in the counseling professions know that "weeping and grinding of teeth" occurs often in this life. No one of us can arrange to avoid all the blows of fate to human life. But the question of how we overcome those difficulties presents us with an opportunity to affirm our decision for God. The question of which "basket" we will be thrown into, the one for the valuable fish or the one for the trash, depends entirely on our obedience to God. This obedience allows us to overcome the selfishness and relapses which lead into tragic dead-end streets.

A woman, for example, who had lost her entire family in an automobile accident was still captive of her own bitterness after ten years. She had cut herself off and lived in melancholy isolation. She complained to God about her fate and had given up trusting him. Therapy showed that in this case the mourning for the lost family had absorbed all the powers of the survivor. She raged on in her aloneness, refused all activity, and hung on to her hard-nosed quarrel with God and her fate. What soon happened was that she began to feel insulted by everyone, and hardened her attitude toward the whole world. The result was, of course, an unforgiving and spiteful mental illness.

Is it possible to cure such bitterness? The crucial factor is that the despairing person have an experience which contradicts his or her assumed bitterness. The person needs to live the experience that she is not abandoned, that there is someone who still stands for life in spite of the inconstancy of others and her own complaining. One way of structuring such an experience is for the person to come regularly to a counselor for talk. The counselor need only listen to the stereotyped complaints and self-pity each time.

After many such hours the condition of the woman became markedly better. She began to open up to questions about her life and her environment. Then it became clear to her that after such cruel blows of fate new strength is made available. Whether this new strength is used depends entirely on the decision of the person to accept or reject it. With the help of a counselor the insight that her decade-long mourning and bitterness was something other than faithfulness or courage grew. She saw it after those sessions as a quarrelsome pattern of childish behavior directed against a mean father. The possibility of this insight, however, presupposes the constancy and attentive enthusiasm of the counselor as the woman again gained courage. After two years of care, it was possible to explain to her that suffering is in no way always fateful punishment. It is often a test which gives the person the chance to say his own "yes" to life through his sturdiness in times of need. It becomes an opportunity to defend God's creation against the unformed chaos, and therefore to work for its completion and realization.

Such a change in attitude resembles a rebirth, or a redemption from prison. With intuitive clarity, Weinreb writes about this: "In the New Testament we read much about the catching of fish and the distribution of the fish to large crowds of people. This has to do with the Hebrew letter *sade,* which resembles a fishhook. It becomes obvious that the fishhook is connected with the ending of imprisonment in water and therefore in time.

Bringing the fish out of water onto dry land is significant in that the disciples of Jesus were fishermen, and were called by him to become 'fishers of men.' "

This commission of God is experienced in the dreams of a number of persons exactly as being in the net or on the hook. A young woman who after a number of false starts in social work found her calling dreamed the following: "I am in water. Am I a fish, or do I only have a fish's tail? I am swimming and making a lot of progress. All of a sudden I notice that I am being pulled. I feel a fishhook deep in my throat. The hook is attached to a long rope. I jump up above the surface and look into the eyes of a large old man, who looks earnestly into my eyes." This young woman wrote a poem about the dream. She brought it to the counseling session. She herself thought, "The old man is God, and I am his fish." Here is the poem:

> The hook—
> how it pulls and directs me
> willessly
> out of the foggy heights it commands,
> but I wanted to be free.
>
> How it calls me
> to swim
> against the stream, to
> gasp as I am pulled—
> And I wanted to be free.
>
> How it rips at me
> and hurts me
> and requires me
> to leap, although
> I cannot.
>
> How it lets me
> know
> under the burden of its
> inescapableness
> quietly and peacefully:
> how paltry is "being free."

To understand life as call, as a commission—this is the direction of another of Christ's parables. This time the parable takes its images from economic life. The text reads:

> It is like a man on his way abroad who summoned his servants and entrusted his property to them. To one he gave five talents, to another two, to a third one; each in proportion to his ability. Then he set out. The man who had received the five talents promptly went out and traded with them and made five more. The man who had received two made two more in the same way. But the man who had received one went off and dug a hole in the ground and hid his master's money. Now a long time after, the master of those servants came back and went through his accounts with them. The man who had received the five talents came forward bringing five more. "Sir," he said, "you entrusted me with five talents; here are five more that I have made." His master said to him, "Well done, good and faithful servant; you have shown you can be faithful in small things, I will trust you with greater; come and join in your master's happiness." Next the man with the two talents came forward. "Sir," he said, "you entrusted me with two talents; here are two more that I have made." His master said to him, "Well done, good and faithful servant; you have shown you can be faithful in small things, I will trust you with greater; come and join in your master's happiness." Last came forward the man who had the one talent. "Sir," said he, "I had heard you were a hard man, reaping where you have not sown and gathering where you have not scattered; so I was afraid, and I went off and hid your talent in the ground. Here it is; it was yours, you have it back." But his master answered him, "You wicked and lazy servant! So you knew that I reap where I have not sown and gather where I have not scattered? Well then, you should have deposited my money with the bankers, and on my return I would have recovered my capital with interest. So now take the talent from him and give it to the man who has the five talents. For to everyone who has will be given more, and he will have more than enough; but from the man who has not, even what he has will be taken away. As for this good-for-nothing servant, throw him out into the dark, where there will be weeping and grinding of teeth."

The fact that each person in his own way and under different conditions must nevertheless produce more talents is a call to a worthwhile life. Spiritual fulfillment and enrichment is promised to those who make the effort to employ their particular gifts in this life and thereby make their own potential real. The "lazy" person for our text is the one who ignores his "service" and does not use his own gifts. The related practical question is, of course, How do I discover which talents, which gifts are mine?

Thoughtful young people often pose exactly this question when seeking psychological counsel. That in itself is no problem. Such questions are properly asked during youth. Our talents or our calling are not static and unchangeable, since with maturation they change. It is in fact a sign that we have passed through a certain developmental stage when we re-pose the question of our calling.

It is then, I think, promising when this question is asked at the beginning of adulthood. For this search for an optimal use of one's life, for congruence of one's situation, potential, and its realization is at the same time a question of meaning for one's life. It is a sign of a searching drive in all of us to reach a goal and to complete that which has been begun in us. Even when young people do not know about or remember the parable of the talents or its meaning, life itself poses the question, "What am I good for?" This itself is the beginning of God's call. Again without knowledge or understanding of the Biblical text, many persons today are confronted with the need to "produce something." But the Lord goes away, the text says. He leaves his servants alone with their abilities. It is extraordinarily difficult to do the right thing. The "servants" and the various kinds of people in our world today show that there are a variety of results at life's end. Two produced something, the third did not. This result, which depicts a lack of the proper use of one's gifts, indicates that human beings need help as they search. For one's gifts are of no avail unless they are recognized. This recognition is made more difficult by the reduction and throttling of several vital impulses in the children of our day. In such a situation it can happen that these unsatisfied impulses thrust themselves into the foreground and childishly determine an adult's calling. I experienced it in this way one day. A youth who had already been imprisoned for theft wanted absolutely to become a "baker of sweets," as he put it. His theft and his vocational desire developed out of the same source. He had an irresistible longing to possess "something sweet," which had been kept from him as a child. After psychotherapeutic healing of his addiction to stealing, he changed his thoughts about his vocation too. He discovered his real talent and after a time became a successful graphic artist. Experiences of this kind show that the "digging up of the talents" must occur for many people. This usually involves recognizing one's own weaknesses in order to determine the real direction one must choose. A person who seeks a meaningful life in the perspective of our parable needs knowledge of himself.

I would like to stay with this problem a bit longer, not so much as a continuation of the Biblical interpretation as a detailing of how one can respond to the parable's exhortation. So the following is less about the specifics of the parable (they do not tell us how to respond to the parable) and more about some practical suggestions from my counseling practice.

The question itself, "What am I good for?" which we in psychology hear so often, is a help. It is the result of an insight that one's own self-knowledge always leaves the picture incomplete. Isolated reflection in one's own room seldom produces a resolution to this question. Indeed, this approach used exclusively can often lead to monstrous mistakes. One tends either to overestimate or underestimate one's own character. Out of such depressing insights often comes the conclusion that the individual simply must have a conversation partner. However, not every well-meaning person can provide genuine help. The real help comes only when both partners operate with specific presuppositions. First of all, the conversation partner who wants to help must be able to see beyond himself. Parents and family members are, for this reason, often inappropriate conversation partners. Without wanting to, they identify with their son or daughter. "But you are a born salesman," the father says, and neither the son nor the father realizes that this could well be a projection of the father's secret wish for his son. Yes, it is specifically the good parent who can block the child from becoming what it needs to be. Often there is the secret agenda of becoming like mother or father. This ignores the essential need for testing one's self, to find one's own way. The spitefulness and opposition of puberty have at least this advantage—the child will not mindlessly accept the parents' models. The person who senses a need to become clear about his life's calling needs a conversation partner who can see beyond himself. The helper must be able to see the person objectively without identifying or projecting too strongly.

The techniques of psychoanalysis and therapy have proved that discovering one's own talents depends less on an active guide for the person's soul and more on the counselor's listening presence. The conversation partner becomes a mirror or an echo. This allows real reflection in the truest sense of the word. In this way the questioning person's thoughts come back to him at a higher level of consciousness (having heard his counselor simply feed the thoughts back). Basically, of course, such a partnership need not consist of a searcher and a counselor. The partner can be a layperson. The partner must simply meet three requirements: he must be able to see beyond himself, he must listen with care and feed back to the person what he hears, and he must be able to accept the other person with all his character traits even if they are unattractive. A diary can also fulfill many of these same functions by reflecting back to a person thoughts from a week or so before.

Much of our difficulty in obtaining clear insight into our own character is due to our constructing a wall of defense around ourselves to protect ourselves from being hurt. It is only through a relatively stable self-assuredness that we survive our day-to-day life. But through this self-assuredness we tend to repress the negative side of our character. The difficulty then in obtaining clarity is rooted in a biologically grounded and highly justified instinct for self-preservation. But we can receive a somewhat objective view of ourselves when we dare break through this meaningful armor to recognize our particular needs and weaknesses. Only then can we initiate our own self-development process. But it is easier to take the courage to look without illusion into the mirror of our own soul when we also know that we are not the only imperfect and weak persons. When we are conscious of the difficulties of others, our own instinct for self-preservation does not need to defend our self-worth so vigilantly.

But to produce something with one's talents involves more than addressing our shadow side. The work with the shadow side is indeed the point of the parable. But there is more to the process. One must also recognize one's special and best abilities, and then strategize about how to use them in one's life. In this area a helpful criterion has developed. Joy and success act as wonderful measuring sticks in recognizing which gifts can be accented. It is true that skilled pedagogues can make us joyful and successful in areas of only mediocre talent, while another great gift may slumber on the floor of our soul. But there is yet another criterion to help us decide and discover the undeveloped. That criterion is instinctive desire. Simple interest in something is a powerful indicator. Paying attention to this instinct inside us belongs to the basic presuppositions of discovering our life direction. Of course there are discoveries that do not lead to a lifetime calling. Some commissions require only a few years to be fulfilled, and so must be replaced by others. A small girl in elementary school can already sense a deep need to be with dolls and small children. This motherly instinct can extend clear up into adolescence and even determine vocational choice. But around the age of thirty-five the instinct begins to decline and give way to other interests. Many kindergarten teachers need to change vocations around this age, because their choice of teaching kindergarten had been determined by their motherly instinct. That instinct declines in them around thirty-five, and this can produce boredom with their work. This demonstrates the need to change ourselves as we go through the various stages of our own development. The same man may need to respond to an expansive and vital drive to become a sailor, a captain, or a ship's doctor in his younger years and then later as a sixty-year-old withdraw into an isolated house or a monastery to meditate or write. These two very different stations in life can both be the optimal expressions of meaning for the same person in different phases of life. Unavoidable in all self-discovery, however, is the message of our parable—that our gifts are just that. The overarching response to their existence in us must be our obedience to God.

In order to find themselves, many people must make great detours. Only a few people have the possibility of seeing their way from the beginning of their life. That is certainly no misfortune, since "God writes straight on crooked lines," as a Chinese proverb puts it. The detour can also be preparation for good insight and meaningful change. Of primary importance is that we keep the ears of our soul wide open for what comes our way. The wrong way can become obvious in an illness or a psychosomatic irritation. This is often a warning. On the other hand new callings can also be made known to us in reoccurring dreams. Or certain goals for our lives can be determined by encounters with specific persons.

If we want to discover our new calling, it is necessary to encounter the signs and people on our way with awakened and reflective minds. Only then do we have the correct perspective to find and fulfill our lives. Only when we decide that we alone are not the fashioners of our own happiness does that fulfillment come. We need very much to encounter events and persons both openly and critically. It depends on whether our own pride prevents us from seeing the doors that are opened for us through our encounters with others. This overlooking of opportunities is the burying of the talent which the parable describes. The world (the bankers) must work with the talents. We need to be ready.

In the parables of Jesus more is treated than the preeminence of the relationship to God and the use of one's own gifts. There is a third area according to Christ's sketch of the meaning of life. That is the necessity of helping. A good example of this is the parable of the good Samaritan, the man who cares for a victim of an attack on the road. The good Samaritan helps without first considering the circumstances or the person. The text says:

A man was once on his way down from Jerusalem to Jericho and fell into the hands of brigands; they took all he had, beat him and then made off, leaving him half dead. Now a priest happened to be traveling down the same road, but when he saw the man, he passed by on the other side. In the same way a Levite who came to the place saw him, and passed by on the other side. But a Samaritan traveler who came upon him was moved with compassion when he saw him. He went up and bandaged his wounds, pouring oil and wine on them. He then lifted him onto his own mount, carried him to the inn and looked after him. Next day, he took out two denarii and handed them to the innkeeper. "Look after him," he said, "and on my way back I will make good any extra expense you have." "Which of these three, do you think, proved himself a neighbor to the man who fell into the brigands' hands?" Jesus asked. "The one who took pity on him," he replied. Jesus said to him, "Go, and do the same yourself."

We all feel challenged by this story. And everyone who has chosen a social vocation has experienced that it is really extraordinarily complicated to provide real help. For the wounded man in the parable indicates something more than physical human need. The suffering and wounds can also be of the soul. Such suffering does provide us with the knowledge that good intentions do not suffice. Unless we want to take on the role of the priest or of the Levite (those who do not recognize the need), we need to rethink the problem of how to help. We need additional knowledge about the nature of humankind and its special communications problems in our technological life. The following study is an attempt to do justice to Jesus' call to co-humanity by analyzing the problem of how we can really help.

The forms of our life today drive us inevitably into isolation. This development is based to a large extent on the fact that we no longer need our neighbors in the same ways we used to. In earlier times people were directed more to one another and to mutual private help—just because there was not yet any organized help. When a woman was ready to bear a child or when a cow fell into a ditch, or when there was critical illness or fire or war, people were simply forced to stand fast together. Then there was more knocking on each other's door, and more looking beyond mutual facades. This resulted in a higher motivation for mutual aid.

Our highly organized social state has "improved" upon this situation. Only now, however, is the shadow side of this organization becoming visible. The results in certain respects seem to be the loss of human contact and opportunity for interaction. This reduction in the experiences of voluntary mutual help produces distress within people and even a loss of the stuff of our souls. The unavoidability of being very close to many people in one's work seems to produce a need for anonymity and personal distance. Every person needs a zone where he can play and extend himself. The more individual the person, the more such room he or she needs. If this space is severely reduced, any living being falls into the danger of physical or mental illness. Animals with very little room have a short lifespan. Pigs, like people, have a degree of heart disease when they are penned up. So it is understandable that the closer people live to one another, the more they tend to isolate themselves, simply to preserve their own identity. But this isolation colors our need for contact. It leaves us strangers to one another. It encourages us to separate ourselves from public life and to flee into a narrow private sector. We close the doors behind us to defend ourselves from the outside.

This in our situation is a vital need, and for that reason we have a right to it. But practiced exclusively and excessively, such privatism can only mean danger. It represents alienation from humanity and the depersonalization of human relationships.

But even when we are conscious of this one-sidedness and try to combat it, there are new kinds of difficulties. To open oneself to another and to speak of personal problems can also be damaging or weakening to the one who shares. Many people are afraid to speak about their trials—and rightly so. For everything depends on whether one's conversation partner is trustworthy and does not gossip about the matter. If we want to become more human with one another, we need to develop a new ethic of discretion. This ethic requires that we all pay

106

critical attention to defending the possibility of such sharing from the malicious joy which would want to spread word of another person's trials.

But it does not suffice simply to eliminate the resistance of someone seeking help from his "neighbor." The helper also often experiences resistance. This is the not altogether unjustified fear that the misfortune of the "neighbor" could be "infectious." This is the anxiety that through the sharing of another's needs one could become weighed down with that suffering and finally fall oneself into the same situation. Such dangers can only be overcome when the helper consciously avoids slipping sympathetically into expressing the same complaint as the neighbor. If the helper sees the problem of his neighbor as an opportunity for maturation rather than a cruel fate, then the helper avoids being destroyed by his own activity.

But these blocks are not the only impediments to real mutual help. The inclination to help is throttled in many people by their own experiences of having too much asked of them. The danger of being pulled under by the desperate grasp of a drowning person presents a huge barrier to the realization of the love commandment in our world.

The isolation of the person in need comes, in many cases, from withdrawal. This withdrawal is really a part of the person's sickness of the soul. But the isolation also comes from the excessive claim the person in need lays on the conversation partner. After an attempted suicide a fifty-five-year-old woman told her neighbor, Mrs. M.: "I had a basically friendly relationship with Mrs. Z., since we were both widows. But she gave me no space to breathe. It was all too much, too heavy, too expensive. But she had tried so hard that I dared not say no. And then she wouldn't leave. You know, a person is tired when she comes home from work. She would complain for hours about her new pains, although the doctor apparently was not worried. I asked her finally to leave and to go to bed. But she just ignored that. And after midnight when I became more insistent, she acted hurt and slammed the door as she left. I felt raped by this woman. I had to get away from her. I just couldn't keep going like that."

This tragic situation could have been avoided if Mrs. M. had realized that her neighbor's soul was really the problem. Instead of her justified, instinctive defense she could have recognized both her own needs and those of her neighbor. She could have first done justice to her own need for rest and relaxation, and then afterward set up a regular fixed time for visiting with her neighbor. Through such a clarity of agreement she would be able to set reasonable limits on her relationship and to say no when she needs to.

With these problems we can make progress only if we recognize:

1. That the clinging and complaining of an adult is a sign of inner helplessness. These egotistical demands end up claiming more and more time and attention.

2. That to believe that one is helpful when one fulfills all these demands is a fatal error. All our energies can be exhausted without anyone really being helped. This kind of demand is a bottomless pit.

3. That real help entails the setting of boundaries. For example, the conversation which the two people have together must be limited to an exact amount of time agreed upon beforehand. This must be done in order to prevent the relationship from ripping the helping party completely out of his or her own rhythms of life.

People who help should be clear that such a "hard line" does not represent a lack of love for the neighbor in need. The helping person who does the opposite and takes all the responsibility almost always discovers himself to have failed to help in the end. The situation results usually in resignation and disappointment. This kind of helping has the effect of impeding the maturation of the person in need. It encourages either a passivity or a tormenting aggressiveness against the "saviors." Attempts to help one's "neighbor" degenerate into new expressions of need, when they persist in creating dependence. The helpful Samaritan does care for the sick man and does postpone his journey. But he does not give it up. The story expressly describes the second stage, where the person in need must do something. It does not simply end with the first stage, in

108

which the Samaritan is the active agent.

This is an especially sore point for those people who perform various kinds of social work, since the number of people with exaggerated claims is increasing. To a great extent that is the result of spoiling children. This attitude in child-rearing reinforces the egotism of childhood to the extent that the limited selfishness overflows into adulthood. These exaggerated claims are also encouraged, for instance, by the overestimation of medicine's value. The overvaluation of the bodily provokes the illusion that the doctor and his helpers have the capacity to eliminate all the suffering and sickness in the world. When the medical profession cannot produce, it is supposed to be disgraceful. For the continued sickness is thought to be the result of a lack of medical diligence or due to professional ignorance. Our world has repressed the inevitability of death. This renders many of our contemporaries unable to accept an incurable disease and to work through it psychically with the help of religious commitments. Instead of working through the inevitability of death, many patients regress to the state of a whining child. In such cases one simply cannot be helpful. To try to fulfill all the wishes of the "child" only encourages the exaggeration all the more. What needs to be done is to change the attitude of the person toward his own body and death. We must attempt to recognize and accept the limits of medicine. Despite all the progress, the medical people will not ever master death. Boundaries of this sort are unavoidable, as we learned from the myth about the angels' marriages. For we degenerate with giant steps when such limits are not set. This is the primeval experience of people. For that reason it has been seen to that "the trees don't grow in heaven."

Such problems in being of real help to anyone demonstrate clearly that love of one's neighbor is becoming an increasingly difficult ideal, if one is limited to the "earthly" social domain. Brotherly love becomes a farce if its advocates do not have their roots in a religious commitment. It is such an understanding of life as service for God which enables brotherly and sisterly love. For that reason the socialist utopia where everyone has as much as possible with the least amount of commit-

109

ment is one-sided in the eyes of Christians. For Christians that would mean, for example, a dangerous curtailing of this chapter in Luke where the parable of the good Samaritan is found. It is inadmissible to leave off the beginning of the chapter. There it says:

> There was a lawyer who, to disconcert him, stood up and said to him, "Master, what must I do to inherit eternal life?" He said to him, "What is written in the Law? What do you read there?" He replied, "You must love the Lord your God with all your heart, with all your soul, with all your strength, and with all your mind, and your neighbor as yourself." "You have answered right," Jesus said, "do this and life is yours."

Secularized social utopias block this priority of the text, only to fix on the illusion of a fool's paradise which is unbecoming to real people simply because it cripples meaningful activity. For that reason the needs of the soul pour out into our society of affluence despite the highly organized social service apparatus. This should teach us that it is presumptuous to believe that we could discover a system which fulfills humankind. The possibility of having a worriless life does not so much depend on the equitable distribution of goods. Our society of affluence testifies against that solution by its glaring failures. The real possibility lies in being the "lilies of the field," which unhesitatingly obey God's laws. The image of the lilies in the field does not say that we should carelessly and irresponsibly romp through our lives. Rather, it expressly states that our basic needs will be fulfilled if we understand our life's activity as a serious commission of God. The end of the comparison to the lilies summarizes this idea well. "So do not worry; do not say, 'What are we to eat? What shall we drink? How are we to be clothed?' It is the pagans who set their hearts on all these things. . . . Set your hearts on his kingdom first, and on his righteousness, and all these other things will be given to you as well." (Matt. 6:31–33.)

Because this is so, we will not be able to come to grips with

"Set your hearts on his kingdom first, and on his righteousness,
and all these other things will be given to you as well"

the increasing deep needs of the soul today if we count only on the multiplication of social workers, psychologists, psychotherapists, and counselors. Without the attitude described in the text or without a conscious living from this same power the social work of our society will be in vain. Unfortunately the situation today appears to be quite sad. More and more people are choosing social service work mostly out of a projection of their own need for help. By becoming a professional helper, they try to still their own inner needs. There are many young people who are under the dark obligation of "Someone must help." Often they have no insight into their own reality of "I need help drastically, because I feel empty, directionless, weak, sad, and despondent." This phenomenon of the so-called neurotic vocational choice is especially tragic in social work itself, since that kind of work really requires a very strong and healthy human soul. Without unusual strength of soul, social service work is unendurable. Without this there is neither reward nor success. Nevertheless many young girls want to become pediatric nurses simply because they have an unconscious need for child care. Many students in schools for social pedagogy feel left out (in their childhood they did not have the love of their mother). They wave the flag of desire and bitterness professionally because they themselves unconsciously long to have what was withheld from them personally. When such social workers practice without conscious recognition of their own need for revenge against their parents, they shove their young clients toward the desire to hate and avenge themselves against their parents. One can see much of the same projection of the personal and unconscious problems of youth in the protests against social injustice. This does not solve the conflict. Instead, it heightens it and accelerates the personal vendetta against an undefined object. In the language of our text this avoids the sickness. We do not help the sick person if we clobber him and persecute him while he is bleeding. Helping must be what we aim for. Revenge, says our parable, cannot enter the picture.

That of course does not mean that every person who chooses a helping profession is in great need himself. Willingness to provide real help cannot be devalued simply because we realize that for some it is a neurosis. That would be inadmissible. Even if help is given because of one's own needs, it is still valuable. However, we must make it clear that falsely placed zeal can do much damage. We can help people on a social level only when we use the learnings of those who study mental illness. Our attitude needs to be informed by the therapeutic techniques that have been developed. This will help us keep in mind that not very much is accomplished by our own effort. It will remind us of the prohibition against playing with the fate of someone else, while enabling us to respond to the call to carry one another's burdens.

In my counseling practice it is enormously difficult to be of real help when the problem is close at hand. Being of substantial help is often much easier when it is some distant or abstract issue. In some ways it is easier to demonstrate against a distant war than to be careful and helpful in one's own home. The distress of a family member's soul usually becomes apparent only when a catastrophe or suicide occurs. It is easier to have pity on the children of a distant land than to deal with the lostness of a member of one's own family. It is easier to love "humankind" than to be faithful to a person in one's immediate environment.

Why is that so difficult? Certainly in many cases it is an unconscious defense against the excessive demands we have described earlier in this chapter. But beyond that are two other points of resistance. The one problem consists of the danger of integrating people (spouse or children) so entirely into one's assumed environment that they are essentially forgotten. These persons who are close to us become so much a part of our own ego structure that we cannot recognize their real needs. The other problem with seeing the needs of those close to us relates to the pecking order among people. The "will to power" does not exist only in world history. It is a real factor in family and group life. Without being conscious of it, we can give ourselves over to those primitive biological needs to take advantage of the weaknesses of others in order to climb to a higher position of influence ourselves. This tendency is a powerful enemy of the love commandment. Such cockfights between people who live with one another for a long time can only be prevented by a passionate renouncement of such power grabs. This renouncement almost always comes by way of conscious conversation about the urges and weaknesses within each person. Without such a consciousness the prerequisites for real love in a long-term relationship are missing. Also, persons growing up in the family must be educated about their own and other family members' will to power. These younger members must also understand that there is a need to place limits on the ego within a group's life. We need to educate our children not only about their basic *rights* but also about their basic *duties* if we want them to be able to live in community. This is the only chance neighborly love has.

It is especially difficult to overcome our resistance in approaching a family in which one person is mentally ill. Here is an example:

On account of a total incapacity to achieve anything, a fourteen-year-old girl is counseled to place herself under psychological care. The psychological tests indicated a deep wound in her soul. The girl is full of fear. It turns out that she is afraid of a "man who kills children." Astonishingly, it is discovered that here there is no exaggerated fear, as we often see. The basis for her fear is a real situation into which she has fallen. This girl has a mentally ill father who lives at home and who frightens the entire family with gruesome scenes and genuine attempts at murder. The mother of the girl is brought in and asked why she has not sought psychiatric help for her husband. "Oh for heaven's sake," she exclaims, "how in the world could we manage that? First of all, my husband does not understand that he is sick. And if I were to have him brought to the psychiatric clinic against his will, what an uproar that would cause among our neighbors and in our village. Then we could just close our little store and pack our bags. Our children would always be looked at here. No one would play with them. No one would invite our daughter to go dancing and no one would think of marrying her. I can't throw away my children's future. I can't remove the foundation of our family's existence.

There was another case like this in the village. The family is completely isolated. No! We prefer to stay here in this misery and guard against anyone outside knowing how my husband acts. Since he is shy, it is easy to hide his craziness."

It became evident that the psychotic condition had existed for over a decade and that the stress of the situation was hardly bearable for the family. Only after the breakdown of the daughter would the sick man submit to taking medicine. Then he agreed to psychiatric counseling. And finally he voluntarily admitted himself to a hospital for long-term treatment.

I think it is necessary to look closely at this family tragedy and to learn from it. For if the man had been sick with tuberculosis, the family members would not have feared the attention of society. It seems to be a pressing issue to reflect on why the sympathy and ability to help one's neighbor could not function in this case. Indeed, the proximity of family and neighbors seemed to prevent help from coming. Why is that so? And how can we change it?

In order to understand such inhuman behavior, it is important to understand that all of us are biologically determined by the instinct for self-preservation. There is a pattern of behavior deep within us which fights to preserve us and our kind. In hard times, only the living beings who are healthy survive. The species develops strengths through a pattern of natural selection and survival of the fittest. In many animal groupings the sick, strange, and funny-looking members are brutally persecuted and rejected. The group keeps them at a distance in order to reduce the chances of the odd member's survival. This mechanism also occurs among people. How barbarically young schoolchildren can shut out a handicapped child. How cruel they can be to a stutterer, if an adult is not around to correct and direct their behavior. How this animal instinct still thrives in human society is demonstrated by our relationship to fashions. We pay so much attention to dressing like others. This is the unconscious and in some ways justified wish to not stand out and be isolated.

This "outlawing" of the mentally ill and their families is a much more crass, yet invisible example of the same tendency.

The primitive human pushes the behavior of the mentally ill out of his world. What threatens is rejected. And with some justification the primitive mind includes the family of the mentally ill person in the rejection. There is a fear that the mental illness is in some way "infectious." Without anything ever becoming conscious, the designated house is defamed and isolated. Our avoidance of the mentally ill is related to the "animal in people." It has no connection with the possibility of brotherly love. Above all, our avoidance becomes real guilt when we examine the new and deep disturbances that result. The daughter's illness is a good example. Scientists are today not nearly as sure as they were several years ago that mental illness is basically a hereditary disease. The illness is also passed on by the continual traumatization of the children generation after generation. Psychically ill persons can mean danger for society. Through their own sophisticated and congenial gifts, the elimination of what was once thought to be hereditarily determined can be contemplated. In recent years the medical treatment of the mentally ill has been much aided by the development of effective pharmaceuticals. Now a number of cyclical mental illnesses can at least be interrupted by the doctor's prescription. No, the mentally ill are no longer the hidden and hopeless cases we once thought them to be.

In order for such a family to come for help, they desperately need the human and compassionate understanding of their neighbors, friends, and acquaintances.

Christ taught us that a person has the duty to grow beyond the barbaric and natural in and around him. Today, with the help of reason and science, we have the opportunity to reflect on and plan for the survival of this ennobled species. But we will only be able to see humankind mature if we bring the animal instincts in people into our consciousness. In this way we free ourselves from the unthinking rule of the self-preservation instinct. We become persons when we are able to direct ourselves to a new and human calling. That calling is the love of our fellow human beings. They are our brothers and sisters. And they are the weak, the outsiders, and the sick—no matter how repulsive the sickness.

8.

Psychic Healing
and Religious Renewal

Very often after a psychically ill person has solved most of his inner difficulties, an opening toward religious feeling occurs. This happens quite consistently without any prompting. In many cases this uncalled-for religious rebirth is precipitated by dreams. It is as if the new steps into health bring with them an ability to experience the world in religious categories. The breaking down of the barriers of the soul seems to free one's religious sensitivities. The psychic healing resembles a process of differentiation between the substantial and the inconsequential. It is like the finding of the pearl, the discovery of life as service. Psychically ill persons revolve around themselves in a tormented fashion. All their thoughts are about their own problems and pains. Their cure is for them an experience of rebirth by "water and the spirit," because they finally gained the ability to look beyond their own sick egotism.

Here is an example: Hannelore came looking for me of her own volition. She had been a secretary for quite some time in an office and she lived with her mother—the only child still at home. Her father had died when Hannelore was nine. She told me that she felt lame and empty. It was difficult for her to understand the cheerfulness of her colleagues at work and it was nearly impossible to be cheerful herself. She very quickly felt insulted by them and therefore had great difficulties in not relating to them as enemies. She was also tormented by a noteworthy habit. She could always count on being disturbed by the occurrence of an uneven number.

Since Hannelore intensely desired to put these difficulties behind her, she came regularly to me for three years. She reported her problems in her daily life and in her childhood. She recounted a great number of dreams during our sessions. We gradually discovered that this externally well behaved daughter had many deep and murderous aggressive unconscious feelings against her mother. These feelings seemed to have their origin in Hannelore's childhood. At that time her mother had spent practically no time with her children. Her parents kept a grocery store, in which her mother worked without ceasing. The children ran around nearby. Their mother tried nevertheless to raise the children as "orderly human beings."

Hannelore said: "My mother yelled at me for the smallest things. 'I am doing everything for you and you are just wild. If you were a good daughter, you wouldn't have done that.' I felt terrible. I felt rejected." Then she told me about a related dream. She said: "I am standing in the store with my parents. The groceries are piled up all over the place. But there are worms in everything. The groceries have spoiled. They are disgusting to me."

In picture language this dream expresses Hannelore's loss of food for her soul through the loveless character of her mother. The powers of the soul to live have rotted. She did not feel loved. So she soon saw her own ability to love herself disappear into an attitude of disgust.

As the sessions proceeded, the meaning of her fixation of numbers became clearer. It revealed itself as a defense mechanism against giving in to her murderous feelings of aggression. Hannelore noticed, for instance, that she could remember with horror a scream of her mother's one night. The child Hannelore ran upstairs to her mother to ask what had happened. Her mother explained that she had forgotten to take a hairpin out

118

of her hair and had stuck herself in the head. Hannelore remembered that somehow she felt guilty about that hairpin. During that time she had often played the number game, "How many holes do you have in your head?" She had the feeling that she was guilty of putting a hole in her mother's head.

She also remembered the worship service at the beginning of her school years. She had been one of the few children who was not accompanied by her mother. She had become sad and angry about that. Then during the sermon, a deep need came over her. She counted the sections of the stained-glass windows. Where there were not an even number of sections, she added spontaneously the word "cross." That seemed to calm her. In this way such rituals imaged a protection against the murderous longings of the little girl.

Generally as the defense against negative feelings of hate and murder became more decisive, the moods of emptiness and apathy grew. Hannelore experienced the death of her father and her beloved grandmother without any signs of mourning. She felt "calcified." "Confirmation class and the actual ritual of confirmation happened to me without touching me in the least," Hannelore observed. "Yes, I did go to church a number of times with the hope that something would happen to me there which would free me from this coldness. But nothing happened. Everything just got worse." This lack of expression of her feelings was changed only after she with much passion became conscious of the fury, the feelings of guilt, and her defense. After one of our counseling sessions, Hannelore wrote me the following letter:

"As I left you yesterday, I was pretty calm. But in the bus a feeling of fear came flooding over me again. I thought I needed to get out of the bus and hurry back to you. I thought I would no longer be able to breathe. I thought I was going to faint. In addition, I felt as if my arms and legs were lame. I tried to remain calm. I understood clearly that my body reacted as it did because I wanted so desperately to stay near you. That helped. I succeeded—as you had advised me—in letting the fear flow out of my body. At that point I thought: 'Nothing has happened. I am being carried. I do not know what it is that is carrying me, but I can let myself fall and be at rest.' After a few minutes the fear had been overcome. For the first time I had the feeling that I didn't have to do anything. I did not have to struggle against a feeling of weakness. I was able to let myself fall. I don't know if I am describing this correctly, but I had a kind of feeling of opening up naturally. Oh, no, that's not the right way to say it. I can't really describe what I felt. I believe that this feeling of being carried came from my experience of your living through my horrible fear with me. It was as if a monstrous burden fell from me. I felt eternally freed—and therefore loved. After that hour where I felt that you shared my feeling, the feeling of being carried by God came to me. Then for the first time I had the need to do something good for you. I wanted to return the favor.''

In connection with this experience three dreams followed:

1. "I am standing at the foot of some small steps with an old man. My left foot has been caught in a wheel which has got a hold on the tongue of my shoe. A woman with a baby carriage wants to help me. She tries to free me from the wheel. I say, 'Oh, let it be, I can slip out of the shoe and then get out of the wheel's way.' But the woman bends down and frees my foot. I thank her kindly and wonder at the helpfulness of the woman, and at the fact that she nods to me with friendliness.''

2. "Christ comes out of the sky and down to earth. His beard is very dark. He lets himself fall into the arms of three people, with his back to them. I think they are two women and a man. They catch him. What? They catch him? I thought he would catch people. Christ lunges forward with his upper body. He turns around, facing the three people. He hugs them all. Aha! That's how it is: first people must receive Christ, then he embraces them.''

3. "High in the air we see a Christ figure. It is a crucifix. It is tied to a wheel which turns toward the sky. One cannot see where it is attached. The Christ figure looks impressive and sublime. Shocked, I say, 'O God.' My guide calls out the same, 'O God.' Why did they bring a Christ figure? There is in the city a huge celebration. Maybe it is the one thousandth anniversary. Or maybe a church feast. But then there is another Christ

figure, even more impressive and sublime. Suddenly we are shocked to see Christ holding his right hand, which slowly leads to his head. Again I call out: 'O God, look! They are giving him life.' Christ lets his hand drop, lays it next to his body, which is standing straight up. It is as if he is saying: 'Look! Here is where I stand.' But he has clothes on. Sure enough, he is wearing a suit for work. Over that there is an apron, and on his head he has a pretty, colorful cloth. The cloth is tied at the neck. Now understand, our city is surrounded by the country-side. For that reason they have put up a 'worker-Christ.' That was a good inroad. The figure takes on, more and more, the form of a human being made of flesh and blood. Now Christ climbs down and goes into the forest."

Especially the last dream shows that for Hannelore, Christ is no longer a lifeless dummy. His climbing down portrays his coming alive in her. It shows that the powers of love, forgiveness, and readiness to sacrifice have awakened again in her. They have given her, the dream indicates, the opportunity for a fulfilled life. In the meantime the young woman freed herself from the painful inner patterns of ambivalent dependence on her mother. Now she encounters others in her environment with both tolerance and a self-assured humanity.

9.

The Endtime
as Existential Experience:
A Depth Psychological
Interpretation of the
Apocalyptic Visions

How can we understand the revelations to John? Are they
the hallucinations of a schizophrenic? Or are they the vindic-
tive and aggressive daydreams of a persecuted prisoner? A
psychiatrist would hardly rule out the revelations as possibilities
in the human realm of experience. For psychiatrists quite often
encounter people who hear voices, see figures, hear songs and
thunderclaps, and allow themselves to be led by commands as
a part of their psychic experience. But aren't these really all
symptoms of a sickness that one would normally call "mental
derangement"?

No matter how much these appearances inspire us to justify
some kind of psychiatric diagnosis, it is also true that in these
images there is a distinct understanding of the victory of good
over evil, and of the light over the darkness. It is the portrayal
of the powerful judgment through Christ and the banishing of
Satan which focuses this understanding. If one translates the
mythical pictures of the book into the processes and conditions
they represent, one realizes that here is a simple and archetypal
portrayal of the world and human drama.

The Apocalypse is a timeless and lively reality. It can reveal
itself daily as an inner drama of the soul in the life of every

individual. It has already been revealed hundreds of times in heavy collective fates. And therefore we must ask ourselves if the "little" apocalypse of the individual person and of the peoples are not dramatic anticipations of an endtime which humankind is approaching. In any case, any more-than-casual treatment of the Apocalypse quickly shows one that the visions of John are not sick fantasies, which discredit real prophecy. Rather, the visions are to be understood as a picture of a great spiritual battle which is actually taking place in our lives. Seen in this manner, the visions can become road signs for us in determining our own behavior. In order to make that possible for us as contemporary and intellectualizing persons, I will try to translate these mythical images into our language.

The revelations begin with a beautiful, powerful, and brilliant appearance of Christ.

> I turned round to see who had spoken to me, and when I turned around I saw seven gold lampstands and, surrounded by them, a figure like a Son of man, dressed in a long robe tied at the chest with a golden girdle. His head and his hair were white as white wool or as snow, his eyes like a burning flame, his feet like burnished bronze when it has been refined in a furnace, and his voice like the sound of the ocean. In his right hand he was holding seven stars, out of his mouth came a sharp sword, double-edged, and his face was like the sun shining with all its force.

Mythologically, light, appearances of light, and all that shines are symbols of an inner "enlightenment," of the attainment of a new level of consciousness, and of the highest clarity of the spirit. John discovers himself in a condition of being absolutely penetrated by the spirit of Christ. He is so encompassed by this spirit of love and readiness to forgive and give that he receives a special power of transforming enlightenment. That is expressed by the symbol of the seven lampstands which surround Christ and the seven stars which he holds in his hand. The number seven is mythologically the number that signifies transformation. Seven represents change by recalling the steps leading up to the completion of the change. In images, then, we see

123

here that the last stage of definition has been reached.

Each aspect of Christ's appearance has a message. His long robe is a symbol of beauty and culture. The golden girdle around his chest is a sign of spiritual costliness, of an inner collection of wisdom given to John. The head and hair of Christ, which were white like wool or snow, demonstrate both purity (encompassing warmth and coolness) and the wisdom of what is to be revealed. It is clear that the eyes of burning flame mean that these insights of the revelation possess great emotional power. His feet of burnished bronze express the fiery suffering implied in the position to which the vision calls one. The seven stars in his right hand direct one's attention to a capacity to act and the initiative for change.

The picture of the sharp two-edged sword coming out of his mouth is especially striking. It indicates a strengthened verbal decisiveness, and ability to admit, and the need for a sharp distinction between good and evil. Such clear and uncompromising decisiveness is the criterion of a higher level of consciousness in eras of catastrophes as well as in crisis situations of individual persons. That the voice of Christ is "like the sound of the ocean" and his face "like the sun shining with all its force" defines the power of the enlightenment as the power of a conversion to the truth.

In the form of seven letters to seven congregations which Christ dictates to John we now discover the seven phases of a definite and transforming raising of consciousness. The first level consists in valuing patience and in consciously unmasking evil (the unmasking of the false apostles as liars). This unmasking takes place through a loyal love for Christ and a readiness to give one's life in God's service.

The second phase consists in the enduring of burdens, persecution, and imprisonment. The third is the clear limiting of each person before the Satanic forces. The fourth is the encouragement of education and self-control. As many documents do, the Holy Scriptures use the figure of the whore as a symbol of faithlessness, uncontrolled lack of culture, and self-gratification. To reject a lack of order and untrustworthiness is an essential requirement of positive transformation. For that reason the text says:

> Look, I am consigning her to bed and all her partners to troubles which will test them severely, unless they repent of their practices. And I will see that her children die.

This terrible threat, of course, does not really refer just to a certain woman preacher who was encouraging the doctrine of the Nicolaitans. No, the text here is treating a far more general danger to which every renegade is exposed: corruption is the result of a falling away from God.

The fifth and sixth levels are portrayed in Christ's letter to the congregations of Sardis and Philadelphia. There again, long-lived faithfulness stands as the central necessity for purification, redemption, and the gaining of "eternal life."

> Those who prove victorious will be dressed in white robes; I shall not blot their names out of the book of life.

In the last letter, decisiveness is urgently demanded and every lukewarm compromise is damned.

> You are neither cold nor hot. I wish you were one or the other, but since you are neither, but only lukewarm, I will spit you out of my mouth.

And then comes a challenge to change, a pointing to the spirit of Christ ("buy the gold from *me*"), to a passionate conversion to belief ("gold which has been tested by fire to make you really rich"), and a cleansing of spirit ("and white robes to clothe you and cover your shameful nakedness").

Just as the white color of the clothing symbolizes cleansing here, so the visibleness of the genitals has come to represent a becoming conscious which threatens to put human beings under the control of their own drivenness. Dressing in white clothes describes the process of the ennobling and acculturation of human drives. Such ennobling processes are preparatory to a new clarity. "Put an ointment on your eyes so that you are able to see." This imagery makes it especially obvious that these instructions are not meant literally. The text is not concerned about the care of the eye as an organ. Rather, it is concerned about effecting a change in one's life situation in order to enable perception. In the following verses—as was the case with Job in the Old Testament—suffering is understood as a distinction. For need gives us the chance to determine the real meaning of our lives and to come to grips with our own carelessness and guilt. It is exactly the difficulties of life which can often be understood as the love of Christ. These difficulties are often the way to enlightenment just because they point to repentance. Then others can no longer be blamed. One must look at oneself. This is the requirement for communicating with Christ (represented in the text by the reference to the Eucharist). It is this communion with Christ which frees one from the crushing burden of his insight for complete immersion in the spirit of his love.

Statements such as these are really rare these days. Need as opportunity and misfortune as an act of love seem to us today to be basically barbaric ideas. Difficulties in life are signs to us of the faulty structures of society. The Bible tells us something different. And, as the psychotherapists can verify, that something different is better and more healthy. Without once and for all taking responsibility for oneself and critically examining oneself, we have little chance of surviving the inevitable judgment by life itself.

The promises of John's Revelation which follow this introduction really indicate a completion. As ch. 4 shows, the promises lead to the vision of God himself. They bring us to the heart of the highest spiritual value. In order to clarify the nature of this preciousness, God is portrayed with the image of a gem:

> I saw a throne standing in heaven, and the One who was sitting on the throne, and the Person sitting there looked like a diamond and a ruby. There was a rainbow encircling the throne, and this looked like an emerald.

This is a picture of the highest level of inner clarity. The image of the transparent stone as a symbol of absolute spiritual clarity is not only present in the dreams of contemporary persons. As the "stone of the wise" in alchemy, it was used as a symbol of the highest perfection of the soul. Also in myths and fairy tales the precious stone or the pearl symbolizes the value to be sought in every goal of life in order to achieve the greatest fulfillment. The "throne in heaven" indicates spiritual power. A variation on this assertion appears in the following verses:

> Round the throne in a circle were twenty-four thrones, and on them I saw twenty-four elders sitting, dressed in white robes with golden crowns on their heads. Flashes were coming from the throne, and the sound of peals of thunder, and in front of the throne were seven flaming lamps burning, the seven Spirits of God.

Twenty-four thrones with twenty-four elders are around God's throne. Mythologically, the number four and its multiples, especially 12, 24, and 144, are an expression of ultimate perfection, if they are related to a fifth or a thirteenth. Concerning the Hebraic mystical numerology, Weinreb writes: "Twelve without the thirteenth is a condition of battle, in which God does battle with other gods. As the Bible says, it is a condition of perpetual and unceasing movement. From the thirteenth comes redemption." Weinreb reminds us of the twelve brothers of Joseph, the twelve signs of the zodiac, and the twelve disciples and Jesus who "as the thirteenth quiets their unrest and questioning." The elders who sit on twenty-four thrones with their white robes and golden crowns are a symbol for wisdom, power, and purity. Human beings can become part of this wisdom, power, and purity after having gone through the seven levels of transformation. This wisdom, our imagery tells us, is not only rigid. It contains also the dynamic principle of becoming and passing away, which the following verses detail. For lightning, thunder, and the number seven in the image of the flaming lamps indicate the highest principle of life: the spirit's ability to change. God is static *and* dynamic, our image tells us. His perfection consists exactly in the unification of these two basic opposites.

For that reason we need to pay special attention to the next verses:

> In front of the throne was a sea that seemed to be made of glass, like crystal. In the centre, grouped round the throne itself, were four animals with many eyes, in front and behind. The first animal was like a lion, the second like a calf, the third animal had a human face, and the fourth animal was like a flying eagle. Each of the four animals had six wings and had eyes all the way round as well as inside; and day and night they never stopped singing: "Holy, holy, holy is the Lord God Almighty; he was, he is, and is to come." The animals glorified and honored and gave thanks to the One sitting on the throne, who lives for ever and ever.

The sea is never understood simply as ocean when it is spoken of in the creation story or in myths. The sea is an image for the unformed matter, the chaos, and the power of substance, all of which is limited through God's creation. This primeval matter is not transparent. It is dark and devouring. The fact that this primeval sea is transparent and clear in John's vision symbolizes the penetration of all matter with the divine spirit. The highest goal, according to this text, is the seeing through chaos and therefore the final victory of clear consciousness over the impenetrable unconscious. Interestingly enough, the next verse talks about how this victory is accomplished. This triumph of consciousness occurs through the untiring action of the four obedient, visionary, and ceaselessly open-eyed animals.

C. G. Jung continually returned to the symbolic value of four-ness as central to the human drama. He tied it to the Indian symbol of meditation, the mandala. Jung saw there the pictorial expression for intrapsychic wholeness which reoccurred in dreams, paintings, and other artistic expressions with surprising consistency. The four radiations out from a middle point of the mandala are interpreted by him to be the four aspects of the soul. Only when each of these four aspects is nourished can the soul be whole.

Without ignoring this interpretation by Jung and the theological interpretation of the animals as evangelists, I would like to note that both in Genesis (snake) and Job (eagle, lion, Behemoth, Leviathan) animals can be understood as symbols for instinctive nature and therefore matter-imprisoned spirit. Even in the dreams of our contemporaries we find human drives represented by animal figures. This image of the four continually active and sensitive animals around God's throne helps define the essence of wholeness. It tells us that wholeness comes through the embracing of our drives by placing them in a working partnership with the guiding consciousness. As in dream interpretation, we may pose the question: Which drives could these four animals portray—the lion, the eagle, the calf, and the animal with the face of a human?

Let us consult some results of dream analysis to help us with the question. The lion is an animal of prey. With its giant claws it grabs its victim and swallows it with its huge mouth. The calf is characterized by its big-eyed, helpless dependence. The flying eagle is known for its superiority. High in the air it demonstrates its power and awesomeness with its huge wings. It is also an animal of prey, and has a powerful sharp beak and dangerously perceptive eyes. Interestingly enough, three powerful drives have been identified in human beings which correspond to these three animals. Psychologists know now about the drives to nourish (the lion), to bind oneself (the calf), and to aggress (the eagle).

Aided by the definition of neuroses and practical psychotherapeutic work with children, we discover more about the significance of these animals in the text. These "animals" must develop within the first five years of a person's inner life if that person is later to be able to meet successfully his own adult needs and duties. And this does not only refer to a person's ability to find and prepare his own food, to define and defend his own territory, and to learn through his dependence on his mother conscientious commitment to others.

These "animals" shape basic functions of the person. They enable one later to attack a matter measuredly in order to

129

master it. They prepare one for the relational task of binding oneself to another person and of feeling responsible for that person. They empower one for situations which call for determination and keen differentiation. After twenty years of practical experience, we know that "fixations" on the corresponding drives develop precisely in those adults whose early development of the drives was hindered. This kind of psychological damage which results in phenomena such as overeating, recluse-like life-style, or unquenchable thirst for power also teaches us something. Here we learn that even if a person grows beyond complete captivation by his drives, he still unavoidably needs the "worshiping animals," which our text describes. The vital functions which they shape are indispensable, because the spirit requires matter in order to reveal itself.

In interpreting the animals I have described only the three that are recognizable. The "animal with a human face" cannot be interpreted in the same manner. Confronted with this mystery, I can do little else than attempt some original interpretation.

Of all the animals the ape has a face most like that of a human. A passage in the Old Testament indicates an acquaintance with apes in ancient Palestine. In II Chron. 9:21 there is a report about the ships of Solomon which came from Tarshish. Every three years, the passage notes, the ships came home laden with gold, silver, ivory, apes, and baboons. We may also ask whether it was known at the time of John that the ape was honored in India as a holy animal of sexuality and as a symbol of the procreative power. But even if that is not the case, the particular appearance of apes in contemporary dreams reveals the ape as a symbol of sexuality. On the one hand this can be explained by the fact that the propagation of the ape, as is also the case with humans, is connected to the ovulation of the female rather than to the time of the year.

In addition, we psychagogues experience that the use of apes by young people in their drawings is quite consistently related to their sexual problems. So it is plausible to consider the animal with a human face as a symbol of the sexual drive. The contrast of the beastly and the human is especially observable in the sexual realm. In this way the humanization of that

130

raw and powerful drive and its transformation into love becomes a matter that really has much to do with the "face." "Looking" is central in the choice of childhood partners during the oedipal stage. And the experience of love in sexual union is, for human beings, a process of new and fundamental knowing. There the ego is transcended and a new level of consciousness is attained. For good reason, then, we read in Genesis, "And Adam knew his wife." In the language of the Bible, sexuality is often the symbolic representation of the attainment of a new level of knowledge and consciousness.

The four animals around God's throne are therefore a symbol both of a higher cosmic truth and of the intrapsychic structure of human beings.

On the basis of this interpretation the other aspects of the text become explainable. The six wings of the animals lead to a further characterization of the psychic functions. The number six is a mythological symbol for givenness, for the arresting of matter. Wings are mythologically symbolic of the spirit. One could interpret in the following manner: these drives can make the divine presence real in matter if they are in the service of and integrated by that same divinity. Only when this happens does the animal in human beings become something other than a demonic danger. At that point the animal raises our ability to know to a visionary level, represented here by the picture of the animal with "eyes all the way round as well as inside." To prove that this interpretation is not arbitrary, I need only refer to my experiences with the mentally ill. People whose basic drives have been mutilated during the early stages of development are always "shortsighted" and weak-minded in appearance, even though they are often both intelligent and experienced. They "can't see the forest for the trees." They are rigid and they continually repeat mistakes.

People who, for instance, did not develop the "calf" of their souls (who did not have the experience of being bound over a long period of time to the same guardian) are stunted in their ability to listen to or even notice that which is in or around them. People in whom the feeling of independence, freedom, overview, and discrimination of the "eagle" is not developed

131

suffer from a narrowing of their perspective. They see every-thing as part of their own feeling of being oppressed. Because of this narrowness, their reactions are often unmeasured and unrealistic, begrudging and tending toward arrogance. For these individuals there is no joining of the four basic drives in a wholeness, like the one that ch. 4 expresses in its picture of the divine stone.

But the picture is not complete. In ch. 5 we are shown that even when the "four animals" are complete, when God is recognized as the highest value, and when all areas of life (the twelve elders) serve God, a person still cannot of his own power come to a knowledge of God's will. This is stated in the image of the book with the seven seals which God holds in his hand. The integration of human drives in service to God can only be achieved with the help of the "slaughtered Lamb."

Then I saw, standing between the throne with its four animals and the circle of the elders, a Lamb that seemed to have been sac-rificed; it had seven horns, and it had seven eyes, which are the seven Spirits God has sent out all over the world. The Lamb came forward to take the scroll from the right hand of the One sitting on the throne, and when he took it, the four animals prostrated them-selves before him and with them the twenty-four elders; each one of them was holding a harp and had a golden bowl full of incense made of the prayers of the saints. They sang a new hymn: "You are worthy to take the scroll and break the seals of it, because you were sacrificed, and with your blood you bought men for God of every race, language, people, and nation and made them a line of kings and priests to serve our God and to rule the world." In my vision I heard the sound of an immense number of angels gathered round the throne and the animals and the elders; there were ten thousand times ten thousand of them and thousands upon thou-sands shouting, "The Lamb that was slaughtered is worthy to be given power, riches, wisdom, strength, honor, glory, and blessing."

There is no difficulty in seeing this lamb as the crucified Christ. But it is important to take this image under the magnifying glass. For in the image itself we discover come crucial characteristics of the Savior. The "slaughtered Lamb" of ch. 5 has seven horns and seven eyes. What can we discover about this lamb through association? The lamb is a young animal which is valued especially for its soft, white wool. In the spring festival of the Jews, the Passover, it was used as the sacrificial animal.

The lamb is a symbol of innocence, of the sacrificial victim. But it is, at the same time, the symbol of a renewal of strength through embodiment. In this symbolism we recognize the ideal of the resurrection, of return to innocence and purity through readiness to sacrifice. Here also we are reminded of the Lord's Supper, where the integration of the healing spirit comes through a symbolic embodiment.

But we should not overlook the fact that Christ is described here as an animal. Indeed, he is not a normal lamb, but one with seven horns and seven eyes. In this symbolism is the knowledge that God's spirit has manifested itself in "animal" life. This kind of life is white and tender, like a lamb. But that does not mean it is without weapons, knowledge, or ability to change. On the contrary, the eyes, the horns, and the number seven tell us of this life's ability to defend itself, to perceive things clearly, and to change.

This spirit of the lamb can effect genuine learning, as we see in ch. 6 in the picture of the opening by Christ of the seals of the mysterious book in God's hand.

Yes, everything is pointing in our "translation" to the revelation of the wisdom in the sealed book. These revelations are in such a code that the most eager experts have become frustrated. One by one, the four animals around God's throne call four riders on differently colored horses. The first one brings victory, the second war, the third rising cost, and the fourth death for one fourth of the earth's population. The text puts it this way:

Then I saw the Lamb break one of the seven seals and I heard one of the four animals shout in a voice like thunder, "Come." Immediately a white horse appeared and the rider on it was holding a bow; he was given the victor's crown and he went from victory to victory. When he broke the second seal, I heard a second animal shout, "Come." And out came another horse, bright red, and its rider was given this duty: to take away peace from the earth and set people killing each other. He was given a huge sword. When he broke the third seal, I heard the third animal shout, "Come." Immediately a black horse appeared and its rider was holding a pair of scales, and I seemed to hear a voice shout from among the four animals and say, "A ration of corn for a day's wages and three rations of barley for a day's wages, but do not tamper with the oil or the wine." When he broke the fourth seal, I heard the voice of the fourth animal shout, "Come." Immediately another horse appeared, deathly pale, and its rider was called Plague, and Hades followed at his heels. They were given authority over a quarter of the earth, to kill by the sword, by famine, by plague and wild beasts.

What do these images mean? What kind of fate hangs over humankind, according to this text? I believe that these extraordinary pictures contain several fundamental statements in the distinctions they make between the bright and crowned rider of victory and the other dark and deadly elements. These four riders direct us toward the need to distinguish good from evil. They emphasize the division between victory and defeat and characterize God as one who decides. The white rider and his crown are indications of the power of the purified spirit. His bow characterizes this stance as purposeful, fierce, and decisive. In contrast, the red rider wants us to consider unbounded aggression. The rider is the symbol of the murderous spirit of attack. The black rider indicates an unlimited desire to possess. The rider on the deathly pale horse announces material death through an increase of aggression, sickness, and materialist spirit (the wild animals).

All this appears to me to have a very special meaning in depth psychology, especially as it relates to the initiation of the events by the four divine animals. We could well say that the "animals" (the drives) in us help us either to triumph through or be defeated by matter. We can be eaten by the "wild beasts." That is, we can become slaves to the demonic instincts within us. Or we can become "victorious." The probability of the latter's happening seems small. For most of the vision deals with the dangers. The smaller portion of creation belongs to the bright spirit (the white rider). The dark and deadly regions, our images tell us, are in some ways more prevalent and produce awesome needs within us. But the final victory is achieved by the virtuous spirit. The white rider is a symbol of the purposefulness of creation, as his bow indicates with special appropriateness. The bow serves the Holy Spirit. The Holy Spirit is characterized by love, creative ordering, and faithfulness to life's duties.

Aggression, lust, and materialism, the three dark riders tell us, do more than make people unhappy. They kill them and create for them a kind of hell on earth. Every criminal or gold-monger or desirer of power or pervert can confirm and demonstrate the horrible unhappiness of such personality developments. The misery of such situations really resembles hell.

Three further insights about the opening of the seven seals follow the visions of the four riders. Behind the fifth seal we discover a moaning crowd of Christians who were persecuted and judged because of their faith. God's answer to their moan was that they had to wait "until the roll was complete and their fellow servants and brothers had been killed just as they had been." In general, this seal contains the insight that physical death cannot be compared with the death of the soul. It promises that faithfulness to God in the face of death produces the opportunity for spiritual renewal.

The sixth seal consists of the other side of the coin of promise. While the fifth seal is directed to the Christians, the sixth seal speaks of the destruction of evil in its image of the earthquake.

> In my vision, when he broke the sixth seal, there was a violent earthquake and the sun went as black as coarse sackcloth; the moon turned red as blood all over and the stars of the sky fell onto the earth like figs dropping from a fig tree when a high wind shakes it; the sky disappeared like a scroll rolling up and all the mountains and islands were shaken from their places. Then all the earthly rulers, the governors and the commanders, the rich people and the men of influence, the whole population, slaves and citizens, took to the mountains to hide in caves and among the rocks. They said

to the mountains and the rocks, "Fall on us and hide us away from the One who sits on the throne and from the anger of the Lamb. For the Great Day of his anger has come, and who can survive it?"

Basically the first four seals are once more concretized and the break between good and evil is underlined. In regard to the fifth and sixth seals there is no room for misunderstanding. They tell us clearly that God will be rewarded and evil will be punished.

The book with the seven seals now reveals a very interesting construction. From the seventh seal spring seven new faces, the faces of seven trumpet blowers. And the seventh trumpet produces a new set of sevens, the seven bowls of anger. The construction of these last revelations of Biblical wisdom resembles an unfolding organism which finally leads to a wonderful and perfect middle point. Yes, one could really say that the seven churches in the beginning are the seed from which a beautiful flowering fruit tree develops. In a threefold process of transformation the plan of salvation is realized in the growth of that great plant, which represents the new kingdom, a total consciousness. We could say this in another way: the flowers in our gardens are living signs of the divine structure of creation. According to Kunkel, the development of the human should occur in a seven-year rhythm. After approximately every seven years, a human life attains a new level of maturity. One can really see this in the biographical dates of many people.

But before the seventh seal breaks into a new set of sevens, there occurs an interlude, representing a kind of spiritual strengthening. John experiences the promise of the redemption and salvation of the loyal Christian, since the victory of the spirit through faithfulness to Christ leads to a conquest of death. This spirit will

never hunger or thirst again; neither the sun nor the scorching wind will ever plague them, because the Lamb who is at the throne will be their shepherd and will lead them to springs of living water; and God will wipe away all tears from their eyes.

This promise is certainly related to both the existence on the other side of this physical life and life here and now. "Never hunger or thirst again" refers to the nurture of the spirit. The promise that the sun or scorching wind will never again be a plague refers to an immunity against the uncontrolled domination of "animal" passions in human beings. In the face of this decisiveness passion can no longer run people around in circles. The power of a steady and loving behavior acts like a living stream for the person, a perpetual source of new and lively strength.

In these images which point up the reality of the salvation and redemption of humankind and distinguish it from the visions of destruction, the theme is always the same. In an almost endless variety the message is that the process of transformation always means ultimate and radical decisiveness. The way to the new kingdom is characterized by the rejection of falseness and the defeat of depravity. It is made especially clear in the following account of the trumpets that only a third of humanity is destroyed.

What can we learn about the spiritual dangers of this destructiveness from the picture language of the text? For the kind of destruction that happens throughout the blowing of the trumpets should be able to instruct us about destructive spiritual attitudes of both individuals and peoples.

The text reads:

> The first angel blew his trumpet and, with that, hail and fire, mixed with blood, were dropped on the earth. . . . And a third of all trees, and every blade of grass was burnt.

The destruction of vegetation by fire and hail and blood indicates the destruction of the powers of the soul through powerful passions, consisting mainly of uncontrolled aggression. Now what does that mean exactly? The fiery aggression of a husband against his wife can burn up love. Or violence by political radicals can lame peace and undermine the opportunities of entire peoples.

The destruction of vegetation by fire and hail and blood indicates the destruction of the powers of the soul through powerful passions, consisting mainly of uncontrolled aggression

This is illustrated even more clearly in the judgment of the second angel:

And it was as though a great mountain, all on fire, had been dropped into the sea: a third of the sea turned into blood.

In the picture language of our text the falling of the mountain into the sea signifies a spiritual leveling. The mountain represents the excellence and heights of the spirit. Through the fall of the mountain a third of the sea turns to blood. That means that the loss of spiritual excellence (the falling of the mountain) results in a damaging reduction in life's power and in a dissolving of consciousness.

Every person is in danger of such a relapse. During the process of becoming, the danger is greatest when a person loses interest in the spiritual heights and when he gives up striving for the heights. But our image of the angel from God makes it clear that God does not want to interrupt this personal process. Rather, God simply allows the powers that have become useless to destroy themselves. For, The Book of Job says, an attitude "which ignores all that is height" is identical with the primeval and destructive Leviathan. When that ignorance dominates, there are times when the creative impulses in humankind are negated. The text describes the situation this way:

A third of all the living things in the sea were killed, and a third of all ships were destroyed.

Depth psychologists know that people who suppress the desire for the spiritual heights also lose access to the depths of the soul, to intuition, and to processes of the unconscious. The death of the "living thing" in the sea, the fish, is a symbol of the loss of one's soul through the reduction of one's concerns to the superficial. But the loss of a third of the ships indicates an additional loss of human culture through the lack of attention to the spiritual.

How are ships at sea destroyed? Above all, storms destroy

and sink them. The stormy sea symbolizes here the chaotic power of formless nature and the formless passions of the person. Taken as a whole, this image seems to say that whoever gives up spiritual and intellectual striving will experience a suppression of feelings. This suppression gives way to a storm of unformed feelings whose violence attacks the ability to form and cope with life. In individual cases this results at times in a relapse into primitive reactions which precipitate a complete breakdown. In entire cultures this can produce a general loss of creativity. For the discovery is very often an image for the basic constructive attempt of humankind to cope creatively with the primeval elements.

Our suggestion that the choice of images in the text focuses on the loss of spiritual and intellectual insight is reinforced by the much more powerful and frightening judgment of the third angel with a trumpet. There we read:

> A huge star fell from the sky, burning like a ball of fire, and it fell on a third of all rivers and springs; this was the star called Wormwood, and a third of all the water turned to bitter wormwood, so that many people died from drinking it.

Again here we witness the process of unforming, of the relapse into chaos which leads to bitterness, need, and death. Here something even higher than a mountain, something more directly "heavenly," a star, falls. This results in the loss of a third of the "living water." Stars are, in the language of the soul, a symbol of the brilliance of the human spirit in the midst of the night of uncertainty. Stars are a sign of cosmic order, an image of the divinely sublime. Looking at and paying attention to the stars symbolizes the human religious search. For that reason Kant says, "Two things fill the mind with wonder and respect: the starry heavens above me and the moral law within me." Reality and religion are meant when Raabe says, "Pay attention to the alleys, but gaze at the stars." By that he means, it is true that the perceivable world is worth our attention, but it is not all. To have respect for the "higher" order is a decisive act for humankind. If people no longer pay attention to the stars, they will fall, our apocalyptic picture tells us. Without respect for God, there occurs a darkening of the spirit and a poisoning of life.

In psychotherapy the text finds confirmation over and over again. Where the respect that comes from a religious attitude is lacking, a person is much more defenseless at moments of crisis. The bitterness of doubt, which the text's name of Wormwood so vividly captures, strikes home at these persons much more easily.

But this picture becomes even more shocking when we go from the world of the individual to the social order. In recent decades have not more and more lakes and rivers become bitter because of pollution? Has the death of the "living thing" in the sea really begun? And is this not a result of a shortsighted and superficial pride? We seem to believe that we can manipulate nature arbitrarily and without respect in our perpetual search for greater comforts. This lack of respect which now threatens our very existence is rooted in our scornful lack of fear of God. Is this not the fearful relapse into foolishness which the fall of the burning star symbolizes?

The fourth picture paints an even darker scene. For now a third of the sun and moon and a third of the stars grow dark, so that "for a third of the day there was no illumination, and the same with the night." We know that this is not a literal description of eclipses, since the darkening of the stars does not fit. No, here the text is talking about the partial darkening of human life when religion disappears. In terms of depth psychology, the sun is a symbol for the life-giving masculine spirit. The moon represents the feminine spirituality which is able to listen, to understand, and to receive. The darkening of these basic spiritual powers produces a lack of decisiveness and an undifferentiatedness. The "clarity of the divine spirit," which both the masculine and the feminine contain, is no longer available. This clouds and veils human consciousness and therefore opens the door to every kind of demagogic manipulation.

How appropriate this image is for us today! We are witnessing today a campaign to remove all "higher values." The possibility of differentiating between the use and the misuse of these values becomes less each day. The world of the day and the night of the spirit which the sun, moon, and stars symbolize here is becoming muddier. Clear insights seem to take place less and less in human beings.

In such situations, brilliant, proud, and lonely prophets appear. These prophets passionately warn against the negative events which are occurring. These kinds of persons are portrayed in the image of the eagle, which "flew high overhead and called aloud, 'Trouble, trouble, trouble, for all the people on the earth at the sound of the other three trumpets which the three angels are going to blow.' " In the image of "high flying" we are reminded of the brilliance of mental and spiritual contemplation. But the rest of the story shows clearly that meantime new horrors befell the unrepentant people.

The image in the next section is very colorful; indeed, it is absurd. The language becomes understandable only when we address the symbolic character of the image. The text reads:

> Then the fifth angel blew his trumpet, and I saw a star that had fallen from heaven onto the earth, and he was given the key to the shaft leading down to the Abyss. When he unlocked the shaft to the Abyss, smoke poured up out of the Abyss like the smoke from a huge furnace so that the sun and the sky were darkened by it, and out of the smoke dropped locusts which were given the powers that scorpions have on the earth. They were forbidden to harm any fields or crops or trees and told only to attack any men who were without God's seal on their foreheads. They were not to kill them, but to give them pain for five months, and the pain was to be the pain of a scorpion's sting. When this happens, men will long for death and not find it anywhere; they will want to die and death will evade them.
>
> To look at, these locusts were like horses armored for battle; they had things that looked like gold crowns on their heads, and faces that seemed human, and hair like women's hair, and teeth like lions' teeth. They had body-armor like iron breastplates, and the noise of their wings sounded like a great charge of horses and chariots into battle. Their tails were like scorpions', with stings, and it was with them that they were able to injure people for five months. As their leader they had their emperor, the angel of the

Abyss, whose name in Hebrew is Abaddon, or Apollyon in Greek. That was the first of the troubles; there are still two more to come.

The fallen star (the disregarding of the spirit) occasions the opening of hell, clouds the picture, and opens the way for the locusts, which embody the evil and infectious spiritual powers. In contemporary dreams herds of such insects stand for burdensome, unfruitful, and tormenting thoughts which allow no rest and which torture one continuously. Often these insects represent destructive ideas which come to people as temptations. One can frighten them away (like insects), but then they reappear hundreds of times. They undermine a person's resistance and eat at him. That is, these thoughts slowly possess the person. What a perfect picture of unproductive intellectualization these hungry, hopping, and flying grasshoppers are! In the second part of this judgment the text departs from the natural picture of the locust. The fantastic picture shows the plaguing danger of intellectualization. The disintegration powers of the intellect are quick and aggressive, like horses readied for war. They carry "crowns like gold" on their heads. That means they impress through logical unity. They are flexible and nimble, as the symbol of the women's hair expresses. They are verbally aggressive (lions' teeth) and (through their intellectual attacks) almost unwoundable. They develop an impressibility (the rushing of their wings), and they argue aggressively and cunningly, thus resembling the poisonous stinger of the text. It is this kind of intellectual penetration which resembles the sting of the scorpion. Now we know that this is a variation of the "old snake," the spirit of arbitrariness. Here this symbol is intellectually clothed. But the certainty that it is this same symbol is confirmed by the next verse. "As their leader they had their emperor, the angel of the Abyss." Yes, the text even names this spirit which the locusts serve. It is called Apollyon. It embodies the principle of opposition to creation, for devastation and destruction is its ultimate goal.

These visions are intended to get under our skin. They encourage the anarchistic impulse in us, that same impulse pushed by the new-Marxist ideologist, who aims finally at the

143

total dissolution of culture. They hold before our society the idea of a utopian socialist paradise. But the idolization of materialism, the idea that life's meaning is fulfilled when everyone *has* everything, removes us from any dependence on the grace of God. This proposal to create paradise by our own scientific powers demonstrates the destructive locust-life spirit of this ideology.

Chapter 8 of the book of Revelation, however, makes it unmisunderstandable that these plagues and poisonings happen only to those who have fallen away from God, those "without God's seal on their foreheads." That, of course, does not mean that those who are faithful to God will not experience need, mistakes, and suffering. But their relationship to God shelters their inner core. Through that they are protected from complete despair. Their soul is certain even when they are annihilated physically. But the people who are stung by the locusts experience a poison in their whole lives, in their spirit and soul. The locusts are not appointed to kill people, but rather to torture them for a long time (symbolically five months). We counselors can confirm this truth with many examples. Many persons today who are fixated on ideology experience a tense and nervous unrest. And when an opportunity to put ideology into practice presents itself, they slip quickly into new sequences of thinking about their basic concepts.

The sixth angel with a trumpet announces the release of the spiritual powers which serve God. These spiritual powers cause the death of one third of the human population through a crowd of two hundred million riders. The text itself goes this way:

The sixth angel blew his trumpet, and I heard a voice come out of the four horns of the golden altar in front of God. It spoke to the sixth angel with the trumpet, and said, "Release the four angels that are chained up at the great river Euphrates." These four angels had been put there ready for this hour of this day of this month of this year, and now they were released to destroy a third of the human race. I learnt how many there were in their army: twice ten thousand times ten thousand mounted men. In my vision I saw the

144

horses, and the riders with their breastplates of flame color, hyacinth-blue and sulphur-yellow; the horses had lions' heads, and fire, smoke and sulphur were coming out of their mouths. It was by these three plagues, the fire, the smoke, and the sulphur coming out of their mouths, that the one third of the human race was killed. All the horses' power was in their mouths and their tails: their tails were like snakes and had heads that were able to wound. But the rest of the human race, who escaped these plagues, refused either to abandon the things they had made with their own hands—the idols made of gold, silver, bronze, stone, and wood that can neither see nor hear nor move—or to stop worshiping devils. Nor did they give up their murdering, or witchcraft, or fornication, or stealing.

The exegesis of many theologians interprets this text as the description of the armies of riders which invaded the region east of the Euphrates and captured it in a very fiery manner. For depth psychology such an explanation has no more meaning than the following day's events mean to the contents of a dream. When we note that the horses have lions' heads, that fire and smoke stream from their mouths, and that their tails are like dangerous snakes which are able to wound, then we know immediately that this is not a description of a real war.

These horses are not real horses. They are demonic, dragon-like creatures of the world of fables, just like many other images of demonic instincts throughout mythology. One could begin to interpret at this point. The spirit of the locust (the theoretical program for the improvement of the world), which has lost all respect, leads to a clouding of consciousness. This arouses one's drives and points to concepts such as "freedom for our desires." When we arrogantly enthrone our desires like this, we rob them of their positive value and make demons out of them. The golden horns on God's altar are symbols of the positively employed bestial instincts. Each horn is an instrument for self-defense and at the same time a phallus symbol. Up to this point they have served nature's order. But their position in the text here signals the arousal of aggressive and sexual powers. Just like the armies in ancient times, a deadly storm of raw nature crashes onto humankind. (The number two in mythology represents femaleness and the ultimate female mythologically is the *magna mater* herself, Mother Nature.) The number twenty thousand times ten thousand indicates a monstrously negative quantification of natural powers. The lions' heads and the mouths of fire and smoke announce the demonizing and annihilating power of aggression and sexuality egged on by intellectualized fantasies. And since these primeval instincts have no connection with a value system or a fear of God, they receive an armor which makes them unattackable. The flame-colored breastplates symbolize the unreserved aggressor. The smoky blue in this armor represents the ability to cloud issues. And the sulphur yellow indicates the corrosive power of the exclusively critical approach. How much the tempting nature of verbal intellectualization is being emphasized here is shown by the power of the mouths which the horses have. At the same time the spirit of arbitrariness and of demonic sexuality is recalled by the image of the power in the tails which look like snakes.

Who cannot confirm this demonic power in our time? We all are witnesses to the trend toward the idolization of sexual lust. This idolization has already led to a pedagogic program. There often children are prevented from a spiritual maturation leading to a real ability to love. Instead, they see themselves as capable sex technicians. This not only results in difficult sexual problems. It also reaps a devastating spiritual death which resembles the apocalyptic proportions of Rev., ch. 8.

Part of our "grasshopper" mentality is the sanctioning of violent aggression. We reason that the destruction of the corrupt system must take place for the good of all. In the name of "antiauthoritarian" education we have cultivated aggression and sanctioned parental indifference. This consistently encourages aggressive tendencies in the younger years. Fiery red, smoky blue, and sulphur gold are the colors of these growing drives within us. The Apocalypse says that a third of all people are victims of the arousing and demonization of aggression and sexuality. This could refer to individual fates. But it can also be a statement about the destruction of social and cultural groupings through the aroused aggression. Civil wars and interna-

146

tional conflicts really do often grow out of a similar spirit. In such cases John's visions speak directly. Little translation is needed where the grenades belch fire, smoke, and sulphur.

But mass death in wars of annihilation can be understood only as exceptional applications of the text. And they certainly do not justify a literal understanding of the prophecy that one third of humankind will perish physically. Generally when the Apocalypse talks about death, a destruction of soul and spirit is meant. This kind of death comes as a direct result, the text says, of persons' placing themselves under the domination of matter, nature, and its drives. This deadly fixation on matter, power, possessions, and sexuality is summed up in the image of the worshiping of idols. For that reason we read:

> And they refused either to abandon the things they had made with their own hands—the idols made of gold, silver, bronze, stone, and wood that can neither see nor hear nor move—or to stop worshiping devils. Nor did they give up their murdering, or witchcraft, or fornication, or stealing.

The above-listed elements are symbols of lifeless matter. If people place themselves under this domination, they become spoiled, Revelation explains. Murder is the result of uncontrolled aggression, magic the consequence of an unlimited drive for power. Fornication follows unhampered sexuality. Stealing happens through the instinctive desire to possess. That means, therefore, that whoever does use the natural drives in service to another perverts their potential. Whoever idolizes these drives necessitates God's judgment upon them.

In chs. 10 and 11 the text's style continues to use contrasting images. After the six terrible visions which follow the trumpets two scenes of encouragement and confidence occur. Through these symbolic visions a victory of virtue over evil is promised. The first part (ch. 10) tells of the face of a monstrous and powerful angel who stands with one foot on land and one foot in the sea. This powerful form towers into heaven. With a voice of thunder the angel informs John of something which he is not allowed to write down.

Angels generally portray the spirit of perfected virtue. As such they are direct and winged (which means spiritual) messengers from God. The size and powerfulness of the angel in ch. 10 demonstrates the strength and power of the virtuous spirit. His position between the sea and the land can be seen as the all-encompassing presence of this virtuous spirit. The spirit of virtue, this image tells us, is present in the conscious and unconscious, in the formed and unformed, in spirit and in matter. Concerning the uniqueness of this spirit there are even more wonderful metaphors in the text:

> He was wrapped in a cloud, with a rainbow over his head; his face was like the sun, and his legs were pillars of fire.

In general, one could interpret this passage as designating the spirit of virtue as being of the "higher" world, that is, of the immortal and eternal world. It is suspended and soft, like a white cloud. But it possesses a wonderful and brilliant beauty, like a rainbow. But above all, it is penetrated by a sunny clarity and wholeness, and becomes the main source of our energy, just like the sun. But when this spirit comes into contact with earth (that is, where it becomes embodied in a human being), it becomes passionate and fiercely combatative. We can interpret the text in this way because mythologically feet are symbolic of one's life situation. Since fire signifies passion for this same language of the soul, the above interpretation is confirmed with the image of the angel's legs, which "were pillars of fire."

This direct confrontation with the spirit of virtue confers upon John the highest kind of insight (symbolized by the loudness of the lion's roar and the thunder). Such wisdom is so overwhelming and central that it cannot be articulated. This is expressed in the command to John not to write down what this spirit says to him. Nevertheless he is allowed to share something important. And that is the news that "God's secret" will not be kept forever. Rather, it will be revealed at the time of a final decision.

The ensuing directions to John are also in the language of

images and pictures. He hears a voice from heaven command-
ing him to take an open book from the hand of the angel. Then
the angel orders him to swallow the book. The angel explains
to John that "it will turn your stomach sour, but in your mouth
it will taste as sweet as honey." After John obeys the angel, he
is told, "You are to prophesy again, this time about many
different nations and countries and languages and kings." Here
we see again how impossible it is to take this story literally.
Even if something like swallowing a book really could happen,
it would have to be a symbolic act. On any level this symbolic
image represents the integration of the wisdom of the book
through the embodiment of that wisdom in persons.

What, then, is this "divine" wisdom which John feels challenged to embody? Since it is related to the mandate to act
again as a prophet, it can be assumed that we are dealing here
with the realization of God's kingdom through a difficult process of personal decision. The prediction that the book will taste
sweet in John's mouth but turn his stomach sour shows that the
insight we are dealing with is difficult to digest, yet full of sweet
promise. That this is followed by a call to preach the wisdom
justifies the conjecture that irresponsible behavior ultimately
leads to rejection in a great decision process.

In ch. 11 the duty, pain, and brilliance of such a prophetic
stance is portrayed in an even more imaginative manner:

> Then I was given a long cane as a measuring rod, and I was told,
> "Go and measure God's sanctuary, and the altar, and the people
> who worship there; but leave out the outer court and do not
> measure it, because it has been handed over to the pagans—they
> will trample on the holy city for forty-two months. But I shall send
> my two witnesses to prophesy for those twelve hundred and sixty
> days, wearing sackcloth. These are the two olive trees and the two
> lamps that stand before the Lord of the world. Fire can come from
> their mouths and consume their enemies if anyone tries to harm
> them; and if anyone does try to harm them he will certainly be
> killed in this way. They are able to lock up the sky so that it does
> not rain as long as they are prophesying; they are able to turn water
> into blood and strike the whole world with any plague as often as
> they like. When they have completed their witnessing, the beast

that comes out of the Abyss is going to make war on them and overcome them and kill them. Their corpses will lie in the main street of the Great City known by the symbolic names of Sodom and Egypt, in which their Lord was crucified. Men out of every people, race, language, and nation will stare at their corpses for three and a half days, not letting them be buried, and the people of the world will be glad about it and celebrate the event by giving presents to each other, because these two prophets have been a plague to the people of the world. After three and a half days, God breathed life into them and they stood up, and everybody who saw it happen was terrified; then they heard a loud voice from heaven saying to them, "Come up here," and while their enemies were watching, they went up to heaven in a cloud. Immediately, there was a violent earthquake, and a tenth of the city collapsed; seven thousand persons were killed in the earthquake, and the survivors, overcome with fear, could only praise the God of heaven.

The first picture of the measuring rod confirms the position of prophet as one who makes important distinctions and separations. Leaving out the outer court of the Temple, which has been "handed over to the pagans," signifies a process of spiritual purification inside the Christian person. The counterfeits in the community should be exposed, the text seems to say, even if that process threatens to decimate the community completely. How could we interpret this image for our time? I believe we can transpose it in the following way: The church must in our day shrink to a more healthy size. Not tolerance, but rejection of the unfaithful is the message of the Revelation to John for our day. Here the only criterion for the church becomes participation in the worship of God.

In this perspective the shout of "God is dead" from the pulpit is an illustration of the handing over of the outer court to the "pagans." During a limited time ($42 = 6 \times 7$ months) this kind of occurrence can produce a negative result. It results in the trampling of the holy city. In this picture we are certainly not to understand the text as referring to the real destruction of the city of Jerusalem. Rather, the "holy city" here represents the central core of the faith. So we are to translate it to mean that faith itself is desecrated when we depart from

150

the single-minded focus on the worship of God.

How necessary it is today to discover somehow the courage to fulfill such a mandate as the one given to John! The continuation of the prophetic vision reveals that strong spiritual powers (the two witnesses) can come into being in order to make God's will known to us. Today's church shows a dangerous and irresponsible tolerance toward the "outer court." There is a frequent call from within the church to work for a socialist paradise where everyone has everything and no one needs God. And there is quite regular deprecation of the stories of Jesus' miracles as insane. All this seems to happen without any reference to John's measuring rod of faith in God. But when one rightly begins to fear these destructive spiritual powers, one also perceives more clearly another, more serious poisoning through this laissez-faire approach. There appears to be a real threat to the "sanctuary" itself, to the most basic elements of faith. At this point it really appears questionable whether such a tepid situation as our own can bring forth "the two witnesses."

Much has been said in the history of exegesis about these two prophetic figures. They have been understood as specific historical figures like Moses, Elijah, or Enoch. I suspect that we are closer to the truth if we do not try to pin down an exact historical identity. Instead, I suggest that we understand them in a larger, more inexact way as great preachers who appear in times of crises of belief. Probably the number two is also not to be taken literally, but as symbolic of the general paucity of prophets in such times.

Next, huge pictures portraying the spiritual strength and range of the prophets are painted. They are God's olive trees and God's lamps. The olive tree, an image in the Orient for life's basic substances, indicates in this case that the prophets are persons who address the basic needs of the soul. They make people aware of the meaning of their life. They remind them that they are "workers in the Lord's vineyards." A person cannot live without knowing the meaning of life, the Vienna psychoanalyst Frankl has taught us. His soul starves to death when the "olive tree" of meaning does not grow up in him.

Prophets who speak out of their experience of God's deeds and existence are like olive trees. But they are also like lamps, because they aid in the enlightenment of humankind. They are known for the amazing power of their words, for "fire can come from their mouths and consume their enemies." This of course does not refer to a real destruction of human beings. It is, rather, the text's image for spiritual acuteness, passionate ability to convince, and fiery enthusiasm. The imagery of the prophets' having the power to prevent rain and to change water into blood indicates that they must proclaim a message which is uncomfortable and unwelcome. It also shows that they have much more spiritual strength at their disposal than ordinary people. However, this strength lasts only as long as their spiritual call. Upon fulfilling their task they lose this power and are immediately liquidated by destructive forces. These forces are pictured in the form of the "beast that comes out of the Abyss," the spirit of drivenness. This spirit of self-idolization can take the power of speech away from the spirit of God's love. This is explained in the image of the dead prophets lying in the streets as a part of the victory celebration of the atheistic "inhabitants of the earth." But the text also quickly adds to the picture to make it clear that this prophetic spirit is not killable. It possesses an eternal worth and is really immortal, as their ascension to heaven symbolizes. The mocking of this spirit, the text's imagery says, leads to the shaking of one's life (the earthquake). This earthquake certainly is more of an indication of the shaking of human situations than some specific movement of the earth's crust. However, we should not miss the larger implications of this message. The prevalence of the spirit of drivenness does also really lead to violence, wars, revolutions, and anarchistic movements grounded in the lack of respect for faith in God.

Our era provides a number of possibilities for understanding the core of this passage. If one loses the handle on religion, one slips quite quickly into a self-righteous arrogance and lives only for one's own comfort. It does not really matter whether this takes the form of "freedom" from monogamous marriage or from pressure to produce. In any case these "free" assertions of self are not able to keep the human soul together. Gentle behavior rooted in the fear of God disappears. In place of this gentleness an unconcerned activism and a conceited unconnectedness appear. But once the unconnected state of life is on the scene, it conjures up innumerable needs of every imaginable sort. For when human beings assert their own freedom, at the same time they discover a need for knowledge of their duties, connections, and responsibilities. A lack of insight into these areas results in destruction. Chapter 11 tells us something about the meaning of these catastrophes. That something is that the way to avoid such destruction is to articulate the meaning of life for oneself and to fear God. For that reason the key words of the chapter read: "And the survivors, overcome with fear, could only praise the God of heaven."

After this decisive and therefore comforting chapter, the seventh angel with a trumpet initiates the central event of the entire judgment. It begins with a powerful vision which resembles a number of stories in mythology:

Now a great sign appeared in heaven, adorned with the sun, standing on the moon, and with the twelve stars on her head for a crown. She was pregnant, and in labor, crying aloud in the pangs of childbirth. Then a second sign appeared in the sky, a huge red dragon which had seven heads and ten horns, and each of the seven heads crowned with a coronet. Its tail dragged a third of the stars from the sky and dropped them to the earth, and the dragon stopped in front of the woman as she was having the child, so that he could eat it as soon as it was born from its mother. The woman brought a male child into the world, the son who was to rule all the nations with an iron sceptre, and the child was taken straight up to God and to his throne, while the woman escaped into the desert, where God had made a place of safety ready, for her to be looked after in the twelve hundred and sixty days.

And now war broke out in heaven, when Michael with his angels attacked the dragon. The dragon fought back with his angels, but they were defeated and driven out of heaven. The great dragon, the primeval serpent, known as the devil or Satan, who had deceived all the world, was hurled down to the earth and his angels were hurled down with him. Then I heard a voice shout from heaven, "Victory and power and empire for ever have been won by our God, and all authority for his Christ, now that the persecutor, who accused our brothers day and night before our God, has been brought down. They have triumphed over him by the blood of the Lamb and by the witness of their martyrdom, because even in the face of death they would not cling to life. Let the heavens rejoice and all who live there; but for you, earth and sea, trouble is coming—because the devil has gone down to you in a rage, knowing that his days are numbered."

As soon as the devil found himself thrown down to the earth, he sprang in pursuit of the woman, the mother of the male child, but she was given a huge pair of eagle wings to fly away from the serpent into the desert, to the place where she was to be looked after for a year and twice a year and half a year. So the serpent vomited water from his mouth, like a river, after the woman, to sweep her away in the current, but the earth came to her rescue; it opened its mouth and swallowed the river thrown up by the dragon's jaws. Then the dragon was enraged with the woman and went away to make war on the rest of her children, that is, all who obey God's commandments, and bear witness for Jesus.

The figure of this queen of heaven appears in countless myths in one form or another. The American depth psychologist M. E. Harding has researched this myth in her book on the "woman's mysteries." She writes: "The Jesuit missionaries found moon goddesses in China and Mexico where no one had ever heard of the Mother Mary. In Babylonia the goddess of heaven, Ishtar, and her son Tammuz were worshiped. Astarte was the mother goddess which the Canaanites, the Hebrews, and the Phoenicians worshiped, although she and her son Baal were both older than all of these peoples. Her name, which resembles the name of Ishtar, goes back to 1478 B.C. But even at that time we know that her cult was already very old and extended back into primitive Semitic times. The Egyptian Isis was called the 'Mother of the Universe,' and all life on earth came from her. Her son, Osiris, was killed by Seth, the dragon of the darkness. Cybele, the earth goddess and moon goddess, was worshiped in Phrygia nine hundred years before Christ. She was the mother of Attis, another typical dying and resurrecting god." Celts, Greeks, and Romans developed analogous mythical images. In the Tarot cards of the Jewish Kabbala there is a moon goddess, whose head is surrounded by twelve stars and in whom the sun originates. And the figure of a divine child, which is threatened by the dragon and which later becomes a hero by killing the monster, exists in countless legends. Probably the most beautiful of these is the story of St. George, of whom the most ancient stories come from the Mediterranean, but who has become a particularly English hero.

Such female figures are primeval pictures of nature herself. This is the *magna mater*. This is the one who is always a virgin, always threatened by a fearful dragon. She is the embodiment of hope. She is the sign that spirit is incarnate, that in the middle of matter a new and higher consciousness can be born. This birth happens only through the challenge of change, symbolized by the pains of the woman. The child, symbol of the higher level of consciousness, is immediately threatened by a dragonic spirit. For this latter spirit, the spirit of chaos and matter, fears the strengthening of consciousness. It is only consciousness which can finally triumph over the ever-present danger of falling back into formlessness. The existence of this motif in all ancient high cultures indicates a kind of unconscious awareness of the goal of creation. All this makes all the more interesting the appearance of this motif in John's visions about the endtime.

Is there here a deviation from the basic motif? Is there an indication of a new aspect of our becoming human? Yes, there is a difference which may be crucial. In our text the child is not devoured by the dragon and then born again, as is the case in many of the legends. This is not simply the cyclical story of spirit drawn into matter. Here the divine child, the new possibility of consciousness, is removed *post Christum* in a wonderful way. The power of regression is lost. The life and death of the person Jesus has changed the spiritual situation. The strengthening of the Christian spirit of love, forgiveness, sacrifice, and faithfulness polarizes things spiritually. It causes a battle between angels and devils. The idea of the good, represented by the angel Michael, becomes such a powerful cosmic

155

principle that the evil, the dragon, is completely defeated on a spiritual level (in "heaven"). That does not mean that the old dragon, the principle of destruction, is out of the picture. In the realm of the ego, on the "earth," it now attacks all the more fiercely. As demonic and chaotic force, it directs itself against the "woman," against the natural order of things, against eros, the female side of creation. The spirit of destructiveness tries to drown the woman with streams of water coming out of its mouth. This image tells us that gushing-out drives can push us back into the chaos of the primeval sea. Such dangerous floods always occur in eras of excess, especially those in which the female principle is ignored. But the image of the earth opening up and swallowing the flood tells us that in the time after Christ the spirit of order is much more powerful than the primeval chaotic forces of the unformed. For the queen of heaven is more than the wild demonic nature woman. She is no longer the gruesome, unapproachable mistress of life and death, who reigns by means of materialization. Now she is the vessel in which the divine becomes human. She is where spirit unites with matter. Through the raising of consciousness she becomes the symbol for ennobled humanity. Her function, the realization of spirit in matter, lifts her up and gives her spiritual powers. This transformation is represented in the text by her being given wings.

The strength of the son, of the new male principle of creative consciousness, also effects a change in nature. Now nature becomes a spiritual power lifted up into the heavens. Now the receptive spirit of the moon is just as important as the creative shining forth of the sun spirit. Nature becomes the female aspect of the deity. The principle of eros, the "eternally female," is now the complementary pole of the male principle of creativity. Out of such an alloying of nature and spirit our text fashions the picture of the queen of heaven, symbol *par excellence* of natural wisdom. This is also the great muse and mother of the arts, the untiring protectress of intuitive knowledge.

Yes, the process of creation now appears on its way. But that does not resolve all the issues, as ch. 13 reminds us. There a fierce battle which threatens creation again is described. And there the author describes the domination of the beast which comes out of the sea, a monster with seven heads and ten horns.

Then I saw a beast emerge from the sea: it had seven heads and ten horns, with a coronet on each of its ten horns, and its heads were marked with blasphemous titles. I saw that the beast was like a leopard, with paws like a bear and a mouth like a lion, the dragon had handed over to it his own power and his throne and his worldwide authority. I saw that one of its heads seemed to have had a fatal wound but that this deadly injury had healed and, after that, the whole world had marveled and followed the beast. They prostrated themselves in front of the dragon because he had given the beast his authority; and they prostrated themselves in front of the beast, saying, "Who can compare with the beast? How could anybody defeat him?" For forty-two months the beast was allowed to mouth its boasts and blasphemies and to do whatever it wanted.

Doubtless here is also a symbolic description of the animal in humankind, and of the associated drive for self-preservation. The emergence of the beast shows that there are times when people lose their sense of the necessity of disciplining their drives. This seems to produce a demonic multiplication (the seven heads), where life itself is governed by impulsive drives. These drives claim more and more of a person's life so as to especially reinforce his drive for power.

What a unique image the mortal wound on one of the beast's heads is! It is healed with the help of the dragon. And the miraculous deed encourages many to believe in this new force without suspecting that there is something devilish at work. What kinds of events is this image referring to? Today, too, some kinds of liberation of drives have healing powers. For instance, the area of sexual drives has witnessed real healing by freeing sex from prudish and provincial mores. Certainly some lives have been made richer by this liberation from moralisms and crippling guilt feelings. But already we are seeing the dangerous devil's claws of the arousal of these drives. For through their misuse sexual disorders develop. The lifting of taboos, especially in the now-brutal sex education programs, makes new needs, passions, and sickness appear. Sexuality is only an example here. Every other human drive (the drives to nourish and defend oneself, for instance) can just as well become similarly demonic and destructive when it is liberated from moralism. The only way to an alternative is the combination of this liberation with a conscious spiritual leadership.

In ch. 14 the consideration is the same, but again with other symbolic images. It is a matter of distinguishing the fate of the person faithful to God from the fate of the unfaithful. Here also the numbers cannot be taken literally. The number 144,000 does not describe a real amount of people. Rather, it describes a state of perfection by squaring the magic number 12 and multiplying that by the completed number of 1,000. The images in v. 4 are to be taken in a similar way:

> These are the ones who have kept their virginity and have not been defiled by women; they follow the Lamb wherever he goes; they have been redeemed from amongst men to be the firstfruits for God and for the Lamb. They never allowed a lie to pass their lips and no fault can be found in them.

Understandably, exegetes have thought a lot about this passage. Is this verse to be understood as a call to celibacy? The improbability that this verse has a literal meaning is indicated by the fact that the faithful are described as men only ("they have not been defiled by women"). For that reason an other-than-literal interpretation seems called for. Therefore we should not understand this image as a description of absolute sexual abstinence. Rather, this is, in picture language, an expression of liberty from domination by drives and instincts. Consequently it is said that these "men" have been redeemed as the firstfruits for God. This is a picture of the freeing of slaves. They become free because they have offered their own fruits of possession, sexuality, and power to God, demonstrating the true nature of human life as service to God. Such commitment could lead to celibacy or to married life, but in any case transcends sexual behavior and requires no specific sexual behavior.

"Virginity" understood in this way consists of an inner attitude. It is the freedom from fixations on fulfilling human drives. We know today that the danger of such fixations is far less when the "beast in humans" is accepted. Children, for instance, who have had to starve and have not been permitted to possess anything often are the persons later who are consumed by desire and lust. For this reason it is of the utmost significance that right in this chapter the four animals around the throne of God reappear. The new "song" which the 144,000 redeemed learn is not a song about a static kind of freedom from drives. It sings about the *becoming* free through the integrating of these drives (see the discussion earlier in this chapter on the four animals). It is said that humankind can overcome its "defilement" in favor of the new "virginity." Our contemporaries see similar images in their dreams. A forty-year-old married woman who after raising several children discovered her own intellectual interests told about the following dream: "I am sitting on a balcony and see all my children leave. They all wave good-by. Then a number of men come and look up at me. They all lust after me, but are totally uninteresting to me. Someone says, 'She has become a virgin.' I am astounded that he knows the truth."

For its own time and for eternity, ch. 14 makes the consequences of this decision and divorce clear. There is either the painful destruction of the soul or everlasting blessedness. For that reason the text goes on:

Happy are those who die in the Lord! Happy indeed, the Spirit says; now they can rest forever after their work, since their good deeds go with them.

And for that reason it also says:

Another angel, who also carried a sharp sickle, came out of the temple in heaven, and the angel in charge of the fire left the altar and shouted aloud to the one with the sharp sickle, "Put your sickle in and cut all the bunches off the vine of the earth; all its grapes

159

are ripe." So the angel set his sickle to work on the earth and harvested the whole vintage of the earth and put it into a huge winepress, the winepress of God's anger, outside the city, where it was trodden until the blood that came out of the winepress was up to the horses' bridles as far as sixteen hundred furlongs.

Here it is obvious: apocalypse can become an opportunity for individuals and for groups, but also for the entirety of humanity. The angel says, "Harvest time has come, and the harvest of the earth is dry." Now we are at truly collective territory. The final judgment is necessary, since the number of those who serve God has become so small that they must be "harvested" immediately. The image of the dry harvest supports this. Nevertheless, one should not take the terrible judgment of the "angel in charge of the fire" all too literally. This is not necessarily a description of some atomic disaster in which the blood will reach up to the horses' bridles. Nor can we compare this text with the mass death of the concentration camps. These visions, we must remember, have to do with the destruction of negative forces, while the positive remain alive and are even strengthened. Certainly here we have an image for the annihilation of the destructive spirit itself. Death in the book of Revelation is not to be understood as the physical death of the individual. The bloody destruction in ch. 14 is related to the rejection of destructive and undeveloped potential through a purification by the creative forces. That is why the angel carries a sickle, the instrument that effects division and distinction. These positive forces help God to his final victory. These forces are immortal, while the negative ones come to an end.

The completion of the cleansing process is portrayed extensively in the images of ch. 15. Next, seven angels appear. They pour seven bowls of God's anger over the people who worship the beast. Seven plagues, similar to the ones in Egypt, follow.

The first angel went and emptied his bowl over the earth; at once, on all the people who had been branded with the mark of the beast and had worshiped its statue, there came disgusting and virulent sores. The second angel emptied his bowl over the sea, and it turned to blood, like the blood of a corpse, and every living creature in the sea died. The angel emptied his bowl into the rivers and water-springs and they turned into blood. Then I heard the angel of the water say, "You are the holy He-Is-and-He-Was, the Just One, and this is a just punishment: they spilt the blood of the saints and the prophets, and blood is what you have given them to drink; it is what they deserve." And I heard the altar itself say, "Truly, Lord God Almighty, the punishments you give are true and just." The fourth angel emptied his bowl over the sun and it was made to scorch people with flames, but though people were scorched by the fierce heat of it, they cursed the name of God who had the power to cause such plagues, and they would not repent and praise him. The fifth angel emptied his bowl over the throne of the beast and its whole empire was plunged into darkness. Men were biting their tongues for pain, but instead of repenting for what they had done, they cursed the God of heaven because of their pains and sores. The sixth angel emptied his bowl over the great river Euphrates; all the water dried up so that a way was made for the kings of the East to come in. Then from the jaws of dragon and beast and false prophet I saw three foul spirits come; they looked like frogs and in fact were demon spirits, able to work miracles, going out to all the kings of the world to call them together for the war of the Great Day of God the Almighty.—This is how it will be: I shall come like a thief. Happy is the man who has stayed awake and not taken off his clothes so that he does not go out naked and expose his shame.—They called the kings together at the place called in Hebrew, Armageddon. The seventh angel emptied his bowl into the air, and a voice shouted from the sanctuary, "The end has come." Then there were flashes of lightning and peals of thunder and the most violent earthquake that anyone has ever seen since there have been people on the earth. The Great City was split into three parts and the cities of the world collapsed; Babylon the Great was not forgotten: God made her drink the full winecup of his anger. Every island vanished and the mountains disappeared; and hail, with great hailstones weighing a talent each, fell from the sky on the people.

How are the dangerous and painful sores on the godless people to be interpreted? Sores, even at that time, were known to appear on the body when an infection was inside. Sores are symbolic of a spiritual poisoning as the result of a lack of respect for God. Even today we can identify many of these "sores." For instance, the neurotic neglect of many today seems directly tied to the arbitrariness of values. Mothers seem to believe that children can arrive at their own inner order and health without parental commitment to their development. That is simply not the case.

Many other ailments of the body and the soul are the result of human arrogance. People think they can trust their own health to the physicians. And countless doctors are themselves proud enough to think themselves as functioning gods. Nicotine, alcohol, and drugs have been endorsed by "people of the trade" so long that one can now statistically demonstrate their destructive character. No, we do not lack "sores" like the ones the Apocalypse describes.

The next judgments from the bowls repeat images from earlier chapters. The sea and rivers becoming blood indicate that the "water of life" (the life of the spirit) is killed. The creative fantasy dies and with it the appreciation of culture and art. The bowl poured over the sun treats the drying out of the spirit again. The bitter reply of the godless reminds us of the divisive and unfruitful criticism of an uncontrolled intellect. The drying out of the Euphrates is a picture of the drying up of creative intuition under the spell of atheism. Here the creative impulse is lost because people become unable to recognize and determine their own limits. The outbreak of anarchy and unpurposeful aggression corresponds to the increase of claims by the age. The picture of the released kings tells us this. Finally huge hailstones fall on the heads of the people and an earthquake destroys much of the world. This means that both individual disorders and collective unrest and revolution result in bringing the progressive process of formation to a halt through a meaningless and arrogant equalitarianism.

In the following chapters these forces of corruption are described again in visions and their final undoing is predicted. Once again, as in ch. 13, there is discussion of the beast with seven heads and ten horns. And once again, the picture of the great whore, this time with the name Babylon, reappears. The text explicitly ties this figure to the false prophetess in ch. 2.

Here again the beast and the whore are incarnations of evil. Again the text ties these figures to the devil, who is described in 20:2 in the following manner: "And the angel attacked the dragon, the old snake, which is the devil and Satan." And in v. 10 of the same chapter John reports:

Then the devil, who misled them, will be thrown into the lake of fire and sulphur, where the beast and the false prophet are, and their torture will not stop, day or night, for ever and ever.

More unveiling of the true nature and deeds of the demonic powers in relationship to people occurs in chs. 17 to 19. Since this is done completely in picture language, we need a "translation." Concerning the whore we read the following:

"Come, I will show you the judgment of the great harlot who is seated upon many waters, with whom the kings of the earth have committed fornication, and with the wine of whose fornication the dwellers on earth have become drunk." And he carried me away in the Spirit into a wilderness, and I saw a woman sitting on a scarlet beast which was full of blasphemous names, and it had seven heads and ten horns. The woman was arrayed in purple and scarlet, and bedecked with gold and jewels and pearls, holding in her hand a golden cup full of abominations and the impurities of her fornication. . . .

"For all nations have drunk the wine of her impure passion,
and the kings of the earth have committed fornication
   with her,
and the merchants of the earth have grown rich with the
   wealth of her wantonness."

Then I heard another voice from heaven saying,

"Come out of her, my people,
lest you take part in her sins,
lest you share in her plagues;
for her sins are heaped high as heaven,
and God has remembered her iniquities.
Render to her as she herself has rendered,
and repay her double for her deeds;

163

mix a double draught for her in the cup she mixed.
As she glorified herself and played the wanton,
so give her a like measure of torment and mourning:
Since in her heart she says, 'A queen I sit,
I am no widow, mourning I shall never see,'
so shall her plagues come in a single day,
pestilence and mourning and famine,
and she shall be burned with fire;
for mighty is the Lord God who judges her."

And the kings of the earth, who committed fornication and were wanton with her, will weep and wail over her when they see the smoke of her burning; they will stand far off, in fear of her torment, and say,

"Alas! alas! thou great city,
thou mighty city, Babylon!
In one hour has thy judgment come."

And the merchants of the earth weep and mourn for her, since no one buys their cargo any more, cargo of gold, silver, jewels and pearls, fine linen, purple, silk and scarlet, all kinds of scented wood, all articles of ivory, all articles of costly wood, bronze, iron and marble, cinnamon, spice, incense, myrrh, frankincense, wine, oil, fine flour and wheat, cattle and sheep, horses and chariots, and slaves, that is, human souls.

"The fruit for which thy soul longed has gone from thee,
and all thy dainties and thy splendor are lost to thee,
    never to be found again!"

The merchants of these wares, who gained wealth from her, will stand far off, in fear of her torment, weeping and mourning aloud,

"Alas, alas, for the great city
that was clothed in fine linen, in purple and scarlet,
bedecked with gold, with jewels, and with pearls!
In one hour all this wealth has been laid waste."

And all shipmasters and seafaring men, sailors and all whose trade is on the sea, stood far off and cried out as they saw the smoke of her burning,

"What city was like the great city?"

And they threw dust on their heads, as they wept and mourned, crying out,

"Alas, alas, for the great city
where all who had ships at sea grew rich by her wealth!
In one hour she has been laid waste.
Rejoice over her, O heaven,
O saints and apostles and prophets,
for God has given judgment for you against her!"

Then a mighty angel took up a stone like a great millstone and threw it into the sea, saying,

"So shall Babylon the great city be thrown down with
violence,
and shall be found no more;
and the sound of harpers and minstrels, of flute players
and trumpeters,
shall be heard in thee no more;
and a craftsman of any craft
shall be found in thee no more;
and the sound of the millstone
shall be heard in thee no more;
and the light of a lamp
shall shine in thee no more;
and the voice of bridegroom and bride
shall be heard in thee no more;
for thy merchants were the great men of the earth,
and all nations were deceived by thy sorcery.
And in her was found the blood of prophets and of saints,
and of all who have been slain on earth."

The fact that we are given a picture of the whore Babylon and a picture of the city Babylon at the same time is the clue to the real nature of these Satanic spiritual powers. Through images, they are revealed to be drives—without commitment, unmeasured, serving nature without question. These drives are pleasure-seeking, ostentatious, violent, and atheistic. Above all, they are related to an unembarrassed materialism. Profit and

165

domination prevail in the pictures of the affluent businessmen in the text.

Interestingly enough, it is not only the judgment of God in our text that brings about the swift downfall of the whore Babylon. True, the unmeasured arrogance of Babylon ("A queen I sit") precipitates God's actions. But God's judgment comes only after Babylon is attacked by the beast she is sitting on. That is, the attitude which attaches itself totally to the material world destroys itself through its own uncontrollable drives. A materialist civilization, according to this text, devours itself. It drowns itself in the seeking of its own pleasure.

The beast, on which the whore sits, is only one aspect of instinctive and destructive spirit. Even more clearly the visions show the beast with seven heads and ten horns as a symbol of humankind's haughty claim to power. On the one hand the beast is driven by animal instincts, just as the will to power is part of the human instinct for self-preservation. On the other hand the beast represents with the number of its heads the quantification of understanding, the intellectualization of a demonic tie between instinct and understanding. That is, the human drive for power is only demonic when with the help of planning, design, knowledge, and science it replaces creation. Many powerful people, many of the rulers ("the kings") have become in this regard incarnations of a demonic force. They have in essence pretended to sit in God's place. They absolutize their own will to power. They are possessed by their instinct for self-preservation. This is why the text speaks symbolically of heads and horns. "The ten horns, which you have seen, are ten kings. . . . For a while they will receive power with the beast. They agree to give their strength and power to the beast itself."

The images related to this beast and its evil kings have occasioned a variety of interpretations. Above all, one has seen in these pictures historical parallels, especially Roman emperors. Certainly such interpretations are possible, but only as a part of a more-than-historical truth. In this respect we need to understand the many utterances about the past and future periods of the beast's domination as the rise and fall of destructive spiritual influences in history. This theme culminates in the often-repeated sentence: "the beast was, is not, and will be." In many different pictures ("the thousand year kingdom of Christ") Revelation speaks of the good and bad epochs. There is talk of the predominance of evil and of the hope of and enduring time in which the Christian spirit has the upper hand. But finally, in spite of the "little time" in which the evil powers are released, the "new city Jerusalem" stands in the text as a wonderful shining vision—the goal of creation.

This city "Jerusalem" is just like the city "Babylon"—one should not take it literally. This is a picture of a time. This is time to come in which God's will and perfection are realized. It is a picture of perfection, we know, since the city is described as a cube of costly jewels.

Once again the stone of the wise appears as a symbol for the incarnation of the clear, transparent, and symmetrical form in material. The stone is here a wonderful image for the unification of opposites—form and substance. The stone's qualities of clearness, pureness, and hardness give us a picture of the powerful solidity of absolute consciousness. It is this consciousness which gives material its honored place in life.

The hymn of the last chapters of the Apocalypse chants the glory of such a Jerusalem, gradually realized through the spirit of Christ. That is why we understand that this city "does not need the sun and moon, because the glory of God enlightens her, and her light is the Lamb." That of course does not mean that one day on earth neither sun nor moon will shine. Rather, this tells us that this highest level of perfection, which the text wants to bring the reader in contact with, is recognizable by its atmosphere of immediate and divine clarity. In that atmosphere Christian spirit alone (the Lamb is the lamp) provides the motivation for people's lives. Only according to the Lamb's standard are their lives perfected. When life is so, then the tree of life, the reason Adam had to leave paradise, is given anew. Total identification with the Christian spirit undoes humankind's need to die. Death disappears just at that moment when the body on earth is extinguished.

> In the middle of the place and on either side of the river stood the
> tree of life, which produces twelve fruits. Each month the tree
> produces its fruit. And the leaves of the tree are the cure for the
> nations.

This tree, on a central island around which the water of life
flows, is a symbol of the vegetatively rooted immortal spirit of
humankind. The picture of the tree bearing fruit all year long
tells us that the domination of the natural cycle has finally
ended. In this picture of the tree of life there is no rotting, no
winter, and no death. The island and the tree in the middle of
it are a living incarnation of the ancient symbol which keeps the
goal of creation before the eyes of men and women—the circle
with the cross standing up in the middle of it. These symbols
are eternal signposts, which our unconscious understands immediately. Somehow they already are programmed into our
unconscious in order to let us know that our life has meaning
and purpose. It is the existence of these symbols in the unconscious which tells us of the possibility of living around the tree
of eternal life. This is true even if we as individuals achieve only
a small portion of the final goal—the "cure for the nations."

Because this appeal is alive in us all, there is today even in
nonreligious people—often especially in them—a multitude of
visions and dreams which direct us on our way. Like lights at
night from a far-off light tower, they want to help us. How
much these contemporary dreams resemble the ancient symbols of the Apocalypse the following dream of a novelist
shows:

"About two kilometers from the beach I saw a wonderful
tree. Its kingly shape drew me toward it. From the beach it
towered over much of the landscape. In the branches about
halfway up I saw three iridescent birds of paradise. I was
shocked to see a huge snake circling up the trunk. The birds of
paradise appeared not to be afraid, simply stepping aside to
allow the snake to wind its way higher. Finally the snake towered above the treetop.

"My gaze refocused on the sea where a monster appeared
out of the water. It was so large that it covered most of the

168

This tree is a symbol of the vegetatively rooted immortal spirit of humankind

surface of the ocean. But soon it disappeared beneath the water again.

"Suddenly an invisible power seized me and pushed me down to the ocean floor, where an extensive fair was being held. From podiums speakers hammered home their conviction that God was dead. Thousands of people assembled to hear this truth. The essentials of the conversations were this: 'If God is dead, then we can do what we please.' Another preacher spoke of redemption through sex. In opposition to this, someone suggested that greater happiness was possible through belief in Christ. A lot of laughter.

"The speeches and responses were endless. When young women undressed in order to lead God's proponents astray, many men became weak and forsook belief in a 'better world.'

"Why did the world become so dark? The beast went down, the powerful monster was like endless clouds which fogged the minds in.

"I saw in the dream how armories were opened. Long barrels grew out of the earth and a single fire arose. Fear overcame me.

"After that, I discovered that I was again under the tree. There something completely unexplainable happened. I suddenly became the head of the huge snake, a four-cornered head. As the snake's head I looked out over the ocean and saw a light figure approaching. It was huge. The sun was its head, and in that sun a face appeared, as if it were Christ. Dazzled, I had to turn away. The face seemed to fill the sky and sea. The edge of the form looked like a cloth made of a thousand rainbows. In the middle was a figure of bright blue. In it I noticed all the stars on their journeys. The figure was sinking deeper into the sea. The sea was rising at the same time, until it almost reached the top of the tree.

"When the figure had disappeared into the water, it rose again after a short time out of the sea and into the sky. Many people, saved from the 'hell of this earth' clung to the seam of the cloth. This was the first time I noticed that I had strangled the snake. It hung from the branches, dead. The sea was red with the blood of the animal which Christ had destroyed."

Clearly this great dream informs us about our collective situation today. But it says something else too. It says that we can come to salvation and redemption only when we experience the existence of the snake, in ourselves and around us. Salvation comes when we do battle against this evil in our own lives, when we take personal responsibility for the battle. Only then does the powerful sun of the Christian spirit help us. Only then can the tree of life become for us reality.